W
                                    YS

7 fi   cts

This book is to be returned on or before the date above.
It may be borrowed for a further period if not in demand.

Essex County Council
Libraries

D0183671

First published in 2000 by
The Crowood Press Ltd
Ramsbury, Marlborough
Wiltshire SN8 2HR

**British Library Cataloguing-in-Publication
Data**
A catalogue record for this book is available
from the British Library.

ISBN 1 86126 311 2

Photography by Nina Wilkie with the
exception of Figs.1, 37, 38, 39, 60, 73, 90, 107,
120, 134 and cover photo all by Ian Barbar,
Pyon Photography.

Designed and typeset by Focus Publishing,
Sevenoaks, Kent

Printed and bound by Times Offset (M) Sdn. Bhd.

Dedication
This book is dedicated to our seven delight-
ful grandchildren: Owen, Thomas, Oliver,
Douglas, Angus, Jack and Cassia.

Acknowledgements
We would like to thank the following firms
who were kind enough to provide
equipment for this book: Axminster Power
Tool Centre, Hegner UK, Multistar Machine
and Tool Ltd, Record Power Tools, Rexon
Ltd, Ertl Company, Liberon Waxes Ltd, CSM
Just Abrasives, Lovell Workwear, Humbrol
Paints, W. Hobby Ltd, and Craft Supplies.

Contents

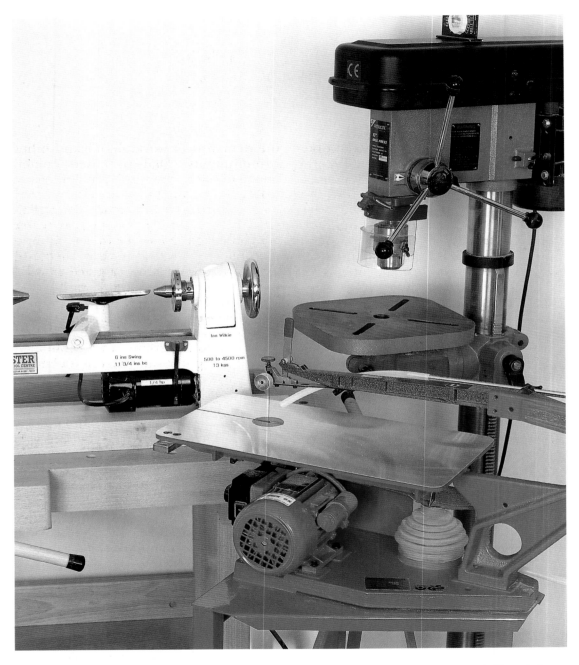

Fig.1 Three of the machines used in the workshop: Hegner fretsaw, Rexon pillar drill and the APTC MkII Carbatec lathe.

Introduction

This book is intended for a woodworker with some experience in the hobby, who has a small workshop and lots of enthusiasm. It is based on our own experience built up over the years making toys originally for our four children and now for our seven grandchildren. It is a modern book using the latest machinery and techniques.

Making a toy for a child can be a very rewarding experience; the toys are as much fun to make as they are to play with! The projects in this book are a challenge to the woodworker's skills – to produce a finished toy that is both a plaything and an attractive decoration in its own right. As we get older we have a great nostalgia for the toys of our childhood: the puppet theatre, the farm, the yacht, all lovingly remembered in a warm rosy glow! How nice to have the opportunity to add a toy you have made to the memories of another generation.

Glance through any woodworking magazine today and you will quickly become aware of the huge range of machines and power tools available on the market for the hobby woodworker. Machinery makes life easier and speeds up some of the more laborious stages involved in woodwork, especially at the preparation and sanding stages. This leaves the maker to get on with the more interesting and complex work!

Time today, we are constantly being told, is often at a premium because of the demands of work, family and other commitments. That promised golden image of life in the future, full of leisure with plenty of time to pursue our interests, still seems to elude most of us until retirement age. Surely it is better actually to complete a project within a reasonable time rather than to spend years struggling to finish a piece of work, or, worse still, never to start because you are worried how long it is going to take!

Do not be made to feel guilty about using machines in your workshop. Beware those who strive to undermine your confidence by suggesting that only the old traditional woodworking ways and tools are acceptable. We are now at the start of another century and we have to move on with the times. Machines are but tools, and the skill and experience to use them effectively, and to their full potential, still lie with the craftsman. There will be occasions in this book where the reader does not have a particular machine that is recommended, but most of the techniques can be carried out with the equivalent hand tools, with the obvious exception of woodturning.

THE DESIGN OF TOYS

The projects in this book are intended to appeal to boys and girls in the age range one to six. The following points were uppermost in our minds when designing the toys:

SAFETY

Most of us would agree that a wooden toy with rough edges, splinters, protruding sharp edges and an unsuitable finish is not satisfactory. Only the best birch plywoods and hardwoods are used in the projects. Great emphasis is placed on finishing the wood to a high standard and the designs deliberately avoid very small parts that could be swallowed by a young child, and projecting spikes and sharp edges, which could cause injury. All the paints and finishes we have used are guaranteed safe for children's toys by the manufacturer.

DURABILITY

Toys need to be strong to withstand the knocks and bumps of play. A toy that is easily broken is disappointing and constant cries of 'do be careful!' will result in the toy sitting high up on a shelf never to be played with. Sometimes it is necessary to forgo scale and realism to ensure strength. Hinges and fastenings are a case in point.

VERSATILITY

A good toy should encourage imaginative play. Some of the projects support other toys, such as proprietary farm animals, horses and dolls, for example. If the toy can be played with by several children at once that is also a distinct advantage.

STORAGE

Today's children seem to acquire lots of toys, and putting them away after play and keeping all the parts together can become a nightmare! Children are usually very uncooperative when it comes to clearing up. Wherever possible the toys in this book have been designed to include storage. For example, the farm doubles as a storage box and will slide under a bed at the end of the day. Some means of lifting the toy also needs to be considered at the design stage. It is not very amusing if a mother has to stagger up and downstairs with a heavy dolls' house for example. It is very tempting to build big toys, but sadly very few modern homes have room for them, and when designing a toy one has to be practical.

The Woodturning Lathe and its Accessories

If you really wish to be able to tackle all the techniques and skills involved in toy making, from making wheels down to producing the smallest knob, then a small woodturning lathe really is essential and opens up a whole new range of possibilities. Woodturning is not some mysterious gift; the techniques can be mastered relatively quickly as long as you start with good equipment and have plenty of determination. If you want to turn seriously and work to a high

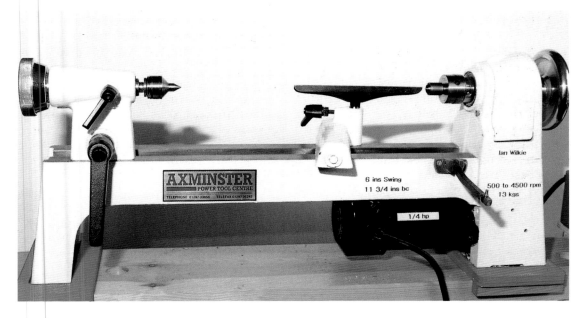

Fig. 2 The APTC Carbatec Mk II woodturning lathe shown here is a small lathe suitable for toy making. The distance between centres is 11 ⅜in (298mm) and the maximum diameter that can be turned is 6in (152mm). This lathe takes standard 1MT fittings and has a headstock spindle thread of ¾in x 16tpi. It has a separate variable speed controller, not visible in the picture, which gives a speed range of 500–4,500rpm. This lathe is small enough to lift and put away when not in use.

standard, and you are not to become disappointed and frustrated with your results, buy good equipment right at the start. After the initial outlay the overheads are quite reasonable, and if you are making toys only small blanks of wood are needed.

If you already have a lathe and some experience of woodturning, you can happily skip the rest of this chapter, but if you are new to turning and have yet to buy your equipment then do consider the following points carefully before you purchase anything.

POINTS TO CONSIDER WHEN SELECTING A LATHE

The size of lathe you decide to buy will most likely be determined by the following factors:

● How much you wish to spend

● The space available in the workshop

● The sort of woodturning you wish to undertake

If you are restricted in budget and space do not despair! There are plenty of small lathes available that will be more than adequate for toy making and some of them are even small enough to put away after use should this be necessary. However, the very small lathes, which run from a 12v transformer, are unsuitable. It is possible to obtain fair results with a lathe powered by an electric drill, and this, while far from ideal, may be acceptable for very occasional use.

ACCURACY

The headstock and tailstock must line up when viewed from above (vertically) and from the side (horizontally). The main spindle must rotate accurately without any play.

RIGIDITY

A lathe must be rigid in construction and therefore it needs a strong headstock, bed, tailstock and toolrest assembly.

DISTANCE BETWEEN CENTRES

Most smaller lathes will give 12in (300mm) between centres which is quite sufficient for all the toys in this book. However, if you plan to undertake more general woodturning you may wish to consider a larger machine which will enable you to turn at least 24in (600mm) between centres.

MAXIMUM DIAMETER

A small lathe, without a swivelling headstock, will usually enable diameters of up to 6in (150mm) to be turned. The maximum diameter turned in this book is 5in (127mm). Remember that if you wish to turn bowls and platters with greater diameters you will need a larger machine, preferably with a swivelling headstock.

THE HEADSTOCK

The spindle should be threaded so that screw-on accessories can be attached and it should be drilled to take standard morse taper fittings.

THE TAILSTOCK

The tailstock should move smoothly over the bed and it should be possible to lock it firmly in position. Fine adjustment should be possible by means of a handwheel, which rotates to advance or retract the quill. A quill travel of at least 2in (50mm) is recommended. The tailstock should also take standard morse taper fittings and be drilled throughout to enable a long hole to be drilled.

THE TOOLREST

The toolrest must be both rigid and well finished as it is the link between the tool

Common Woodturning Terms

- **Between centre turning:** Turning a piece of wood which is held in the headstock by means of a drive or chuck and supported in the tailstock with a centre. This is often referred to as spindle turning and is the method used for turning spindles such as those required for the cot, table and chair projects.

- **Faceplate turning:** Turning a blank of wood held on the headstock by means of a faceplate, screw chuck or combination chuck, without any tailstock support.

- **Distance between centres:** The maximum length of wood that can be turned.

- **Maximum diameter:** The largest diameter of wood that can be turned.

- **Morse taper (MT):** An international standard used to produce a taper on a drive or centre, which when placed in the hole of a similar taper will result in a friction fit holding the accessory in place during turning. The normal taper for small lathes is 1MT.

- **The blank:** The piece of wood that is to be turned.

- **Turning guide:** The woodturner often needs to turn more than one of the same shape – four matching legs for a table for example. A turning guide is drawn to assist the turner to locate the positions of initial V-cuts on the turning blank so that the final shape can be developed. A typical turning guide is shown in the project for the small table. It is well worth the extra effort involved, as turning purely 'by eye' often ends in disappointment. The guide is used on each spindle blank so that errors do not creep in.

and the wood to be turned. It must be in line with the centre line of the lathe when viewed horizontally and capable of being adjusted close to the work, and moved below the centre height, when necessary.

LEVERS

The locking devices on the toolrest and tailstock assemblies should work effectively, be easy to use and should not clash with each other or get in the way when turning is in progress.

MOTOR

The motor should be as quiet as possible so that any noise emitted is not a nuisance to others or a problem for the turner when working. No part of the lathe should vibrate or resonate when the machine is in operation. It is an advantage if the motor is attached permanently to the machine because it makes a neater unit. Switches should be well positioned and positive for safety reasons.

SPEED

The normal speed range for most lathes is from 2,000rpm down to 400rpm. However, for really small diameter work it is an advantage if the maximum speed is at least 3,000rpm. Most lathes have stepped pulleys and a belt that has to be physically moved to change speeds but electronic variable speed is a real bonus because this makes life so much easier. The woodturner is more likely to use the correct lathe speed if no effort is involved!

DESIGN

The lathe should be neat, compact and not too heavy. This may be particularly important if you have no workshop and need to put the lathe away in a box or in a cupboard after use.

FINISH

All parts of the machine should be well engineered and there should be no sharp edges to cut fingers.

ACCESSORIES

The following accessories have been used in the book and most woodturners will already have them as part of their standard equipment.

RING CENTRE

A ring centre can be used in the headstock to drive a spindle. It leaves a clear indentation in the wood, which is very helpful when remounting a blank, should this be necessary. The accessory is safer to use than a prong drive because it has no sharp edges to catch the tools or fingers. If a dig-in occurs the lathe will continue to revolve but the spindle will stop rotating, thus reducing the risk of the spindle flying off and causing an accident. It is worth buying a good-quality ring centre because it will be used a great deal and the point can be resharpened. Note that this is a friction drive and it must be used with a revolving centre in the tailstock.

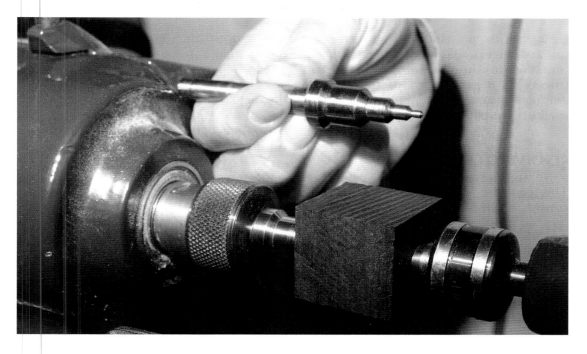

Fig.3 The Ian Wilkie stepped friction drive in use to turn a block of ebony for the top of the traction engine in Project 3. The drive shown above the work clearly shows the four steps of 3, 6, 10 and 16mm diameters.

IAN WILKIE STEPPED FRICTION DRIVE

This is an inexpensive accessory (Fig.4) with four metric diameter steps of 3, 6, 10 and 16mm, available in 1 or 2MT shank sizes. The drive fits directly into the MT hole in the headstock spindle. The friction drive is simplicity itself to use as long as a revolving centre is used in the tailstock. To use the drive a hole is drilled in the centre end of the blank to match the step selected. The pressure from the tailstock pushes the blank against the sloping face of the appropriate step and gives enough friction for the wood to be turned. The drive is perfectly safe to use because it will stop the wood rotating if the turner makes a mistake and has a catch or dig-in, and it has a very smooth

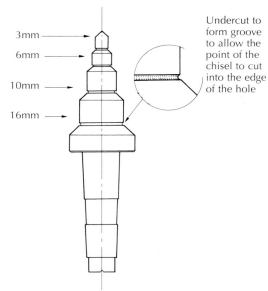

Fig.4 The Ian Wilkie stepped friction drive.

11

— 2 —

The Powered Fretsaw and its Use

The woodworker can have a lot of fun cutting with a powered fretsaw (or scrollsaw as it is usually called in the USA) and it is a relatively safe machine to use. It takes up very little room in the workshop and can cut up to 2in (50mm) thick wood. The operator has the ability to cut internal and external straight, curved and shaped outlines. There are plenty of makes and models to choose from and it is worth doing a little homework before making the final choice. If you can afford to do so take a long-term view. The following checklist covers the points to look at carefully.

● How easy is it to change a blade?
● How easy is it to release the blade and re-clamp it for internal cutting?
● Does the machine take standard 5in (130mm) long plain-ended fretsaw blades?
● Is the throat-plate flush with the surface of the table so that work can pass smoothly over it?

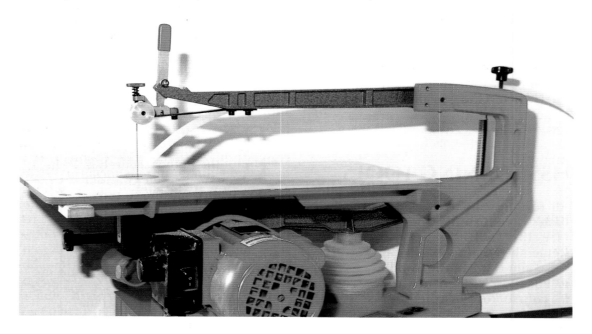

Fig.5 The Hegner Multicut SE powered fretsaw used throughout the book. This machine has a variable speed controller fitted to the front of the motor.

- Is the table flat and can it be tilted to the right or left for angled cutting?
- Does the machine vibrate and is it noisy?
- Does it have a blower to blow the dust away from the cutting line?
- Is there a dust extraction point to link up to a dust extractor?
- Does the machine have variable speed? This is not essential and will add to the price but it is useful to be able to drop the speed down to produce a really slow rate of cut for very intricate work, enabling the operator to feel in complete control. It will also be possible to cut a wide range of materials from plastics to wood and metal using the correct blade. A slow speed is necessary when cutting plastics to stop the material melting and fusing to the blade.

A parallel-arm powered fretsaw, such as the Hegner Multicut SE (Fig.5, used for all the projects in this book) is ideal in all respects. It is a well-engineered machine that will give years of excellent service. It is expensive but it is well worth saving up for if you want a professional machine that is always a joy to use.

ACCESSORIES

Mercifully there are not many accessories for fretsaws!

STANDS

Some machines come with a stand and others have one available as an accessory. A stand will take up a considerable amount of room in a small workshop but it does free-up bench space and holds the machine rigidly. The working height is important: the operator needs to be comfortable, and it is only too easy to place strain on the neck and shoulders when you are concentrating hard. Some operators prefer to sit down when using their fretsaw.

FOOT SWITCHES

A foot switch means that the operator can keep both hands on the material being cut at all times, which is a great advantage. Care is needed, however, not to step on the switch by mistake; it is wise to unplug the machine when changing blades, when threading a blade and at the end of the fretting session.

HOLD-DOWNS

A hold-down, which is also a blade guard, may be standard with some machines. Whether or not you have this as an accessory is purely a matter of choice: some people find a hold-down useful and others feel it obstructs their view of the work.

LAMPS AND MAGNIFIERS

Good lighting is very important when using the fretsaw. If there is insufficient daylight available the cheapest option is to use an angle-poise type of lamp. Specialist lamps combined with a magnifying lens are more expensive but they are usually good for very intricate work and for those operators whose eyes could do with a little assistance! This type of lamp usually has a fluorescent tube and remains cool, which is an important consideration if the operator is working only a few inches away from it for long periods. If the lamp is mounted separately from the machine there is very little risk of vibration from the fretsaw.

BLADES

It is no good spending a lot of money on a fretsaw and then skimping on the blades; they are, after all, relatively inexpensive, and you will find as you become more experienced that you will rarely break one. The newcomer may well be bewildered by the range of types and sizes available. Some cheap imported blades are stamped out rather than machined, and their quality is poor and lifetime short. Good-quality blades are machined.

The following sizes are recommended for cutting wood: 3 (18 teeth per inch), 5 (14 teeth per inch), 7 (12 teeth per inch), and 9 (11.5 teeth per inch). When cutting plywood the reverse-tooth design of blade is particularly good. These blades have the bottom five teeth reversed and they cut the bottom fibres of the timber on the up-cut, giving a splinter-free finish. Two or three teeth must be in contact with the wood at all times. Fretsaw blades blunt quickly when cutting plywood and MDF and they need to be replaced frequently.

FRETSAWING TECHNIQUE
EXTERNAL CUTTING

It is not possible to use a fretsaw with a fence, so at first it can be quite difficult to master the skill of cutting along a straight line accurately. Fretsaw blades are thin, and there is a tendency for a blade to cut 1–6 degrees to one side, which the operator needs to allow for. The following techniques will help:

● Hold the work firmly down on the table, with both hands either side of the blade, and move the wood gently into the blade.

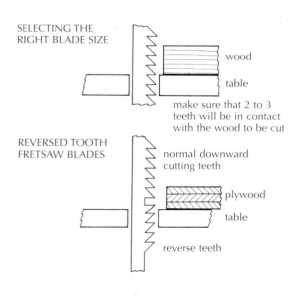

SELECTING THE RIGHT BLADE SIZE

wood

table

make sure that 2 to 3 teeth will be in contact with the wood to be cut

REVERSED TOOTH FRETSAW BLADES

normal downward cutting teeth

plywood

table

reverse teeth

Fig.6 Fretsaw blades.

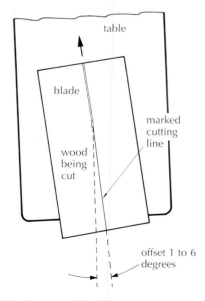

table

blade

marked cutting line

wood being cut

offset 1 to 6 degrees

Fig.7 Cutting straight lines.

- Decide before you start if you intend to cut along the line, or to the right or left of it, then be consistent!
- Do not push the blade to the right or left, which could cause it to bend and break. If the blade starts to go off to one side, ease off the pressure and steer the wood gently back on line.
- If the piece of wood being cut is very small either make a jig to hold it securely or glue it temporarily to a larger piece of scrap wood. This gives you more wood to hold and therefore greater control, and reduces the chance of a cut finger!

INTERNAL CUTTING OUT

In this book you will often need to cut out doors and windows. The following instructions explain how this is done.

1. Mark out the shape required on the plywood accurately in pencil and then drill each of the corners with a ¹⁄₁₆in diameter twist drill to suit a No 7 reversed-tooth fretsaw blade. Drill carefully to enable the blade to be turned so that a clean corner can be cut. Place a piece of scrap wood under the plywood to be drilled to obtain a good, splinter-free hole on the underside.
2. Release the fretsaw blade from the top clamp and thread it through one of the pre-drilled holes. Re-clamp the blade and set the tension on the machine.
3. Start the machine and begin cutting, holding down the wood firmly on each side of the blade with your fingers.
4. Finally release the top blade clamp and carefully lift the work out. If you used good-quality plywood and the recommended blade, very little sanding will be required.

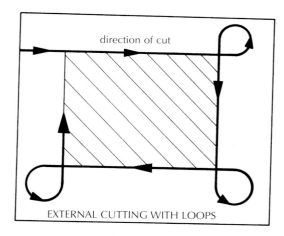

EXTERNAL CUTTING WITH LOOPS

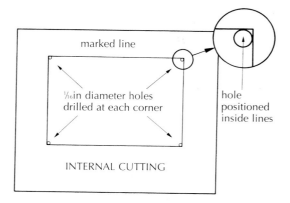

INTERNAL CUTTING

Fig.8 External and internal cutting.

SANDWICHING

Use this technique to cut very thin materials or identical shapes.

- Sandwich thin materials between scrap offcuts of ply to reduce the risk of tearing.
- To cut several identical shapes stack up several layers of ply and draw the shape to be cut out on the top one. Temporarily glue, staple or tape the wood round to form a block and cut the shape out in one go.

17

not so – in fact it equals 6.35mm! This slight difference may seem insignificant, but when you are mixing the two systems, and exacerbate the situation by having mixed drill sizes and router cutters, it is hardly surprising that things do not quite fit as intended! As a rough rule of thumb most material from the USA is measured in inches, whereas that coming from Europe is metric. Woodworkers will be quite used to these difficulties. It is always wise to carry out a dry run before actually cutting a piece of plywood or timber to fit so that mistakes and frustration can be avoided. You have been warned!

TIMBER

Toy makers tend to utilize the offcuts of wood left over from other projects; sometimes this works but in general it is wiser and more satisfactory to select wood carefully for each project rather than to 'make do'. You will notice that in this book we have not used pine, mahogany or iroko, three woods that are often offered as offcuts from joinery firms. Pine is too soft and clumsy for many toys. Mahoganies vary in quality, colour and grain and can be disappointing, and iroko produces a dust that is both unpleasant and irritating to the skin.

Wherever possible we have used British-grown timbers with reasonably fine grain such as ash, sycamore, lime, oak, beech, poplar, cherry, walnut, pear, holly and boxwood. However, some imported timbers, such as maple, lemonwood and American cherry are equally useful. These timbers are readily available from specialist suppliers in dimensions and quantities suitable for toy making. Because timber is heavy and bulky it is advisable to choose and

transport it yourself if at all possible to keep the costs down.

Most of the specialist woodworking magazines advertise timber merchants who sell good-quality woods. These timbers will have been kiln dried and are ready for use. If wood is bought directly from a sawmill it will be much cheaper but it may not be kiln dried. It will most likely be sold in large planks which might prove difficult to transport and store, and leaves the toy maker with the problem of reducing the wood to useable sizes, which can involve some expensive machinery.

ADHESIVES

Modern adhesives are very powerful, and if used as instructed will give a firm, lasting bond. Some adhesives, especially the contact variety, have unpleasant and harmful vapours. Contact glues must be used in a well-ventilated area and kept out of the reach of children. We try to avoid glues with a solvent base. The following adhesives were used in the projects:

PVA

This is a good, general-purpose woodworking glue sold under different names by all the major adhesive manufacturers. It is economical, clean and easy to use, and has a long shelf life. The adhesive is non-toxic and it dries clear, giving a very strong bond in four hours; for the very firmest bond leave the work cramped up overnight. Any excess glue oozing out of a joint should be wiped off immediately with a damp cloth before it marks the wood, otherwise it will be difficult to stain or paint. PVA is not a gap filler so the joint needs to be a good fit and the surfaces need to be clean.

EPOXY RESIN

Adhesives of this type have two parts – a glue and a hardener, which are mixed together. Only prepare small quantities at a time to reduce wastage. This adhesive is odourless and gap-filling and produces a very strong bond. It is extremely useful where metal and wood are to be bonded, and is ideal for securing small fittings, such as tiny hinges.

COPYDEX

This is a solvent-free adhesive which has many craft applications and is certified to comply with child safety legislation. It is clean and easy to use with its built-in glue brush. To glue two pieces of plywood, for example, apply the adhesive to each of the surfaces to be joined and leave for 15 minutes to become touch-dry before bringing both pieces firmly together to complete the bond.

HOT-MELT GLUE

Sticks of hot melt glue are fed into an electronic glue gun, which quickly heats up the adhesive until it is runny; it is then applied by pressing the trigger. This system is quick and reliable, and, once the gun is purchased, relatively inexpensive. There are different sticks for different materials, and for wood a 30- to 100-second stick is most suitable. Unused sticks will last indefinitely and are easy to

store. The glue has no unpleasant fumes and dries almost immediately.

Because the glue is thick it allows even rough, unprepared wood to be glued, and this makes it particularly useful for glue-chucking when woodturning. It is also useful as an occasional, temporary measure to hold wood when drilling, and is very good for jig making. When the glue leaves the nozzle it is extremely hot and care needs to be taken to avoid burning the fingers.

Tips for Using Adhesives

- Select adhesives that do not have harmful vapours, especially if you have children in your home.
- Remember that adhesives will not stick to dusty or greasy surfaces.
- Do not paint or oil an area you are later going to stick something to.
- Adhesive will not make a poor joint good!
- Work in a well-ventilated workshop.
- Store adhesives carefully: some do not like excessive cold, while others are highly volatile.

FIXTURES AND FITTINGS

The modern DIY store is very well stocked with all the bits and pieces a toy maker might need, from butt hinges to plastic wheels. A browse in the fittings section is often quite a surprise! Some of the more unusual requirements, such as exceptionally small hinges, small magnets or

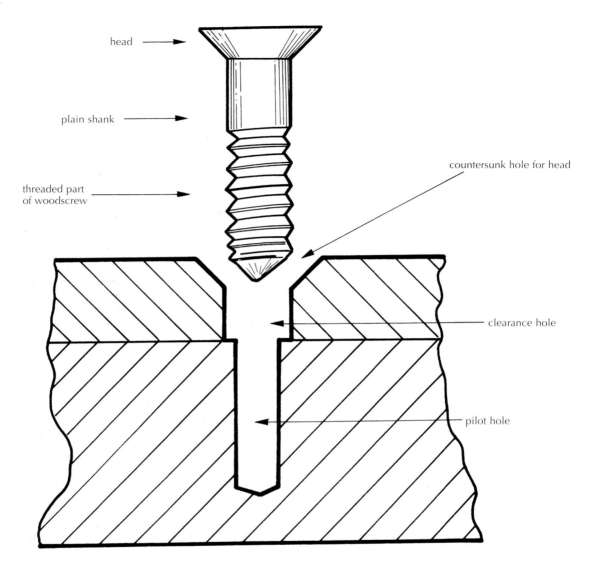

head

plain shank

threaded part
of woodscrew

countersunk hole for head

clearance hole

pilot hole

METRIC WOODSCREW SIZES

Gauge	Metric equivalent (mm)	Clearance hole (mm)	Pilot hole (mm)
4	3	3	1.5
6	3.5	3.5	2
8	4	4	2.5
10	5	5	3

Fig. 20 Woodscrews.

reverse-toothed fretsaw blades may have to be sent for. Specialist firms who publish a useful catalogue and offer an efficient mail order service are listed on pages 157–8.

WOODSCREWS

The diameter of a woodscrew is indicated by a number (the gauge); the smaller the number, the smaller the diameter. For example, 4 gauge indicates a screw of ⅛in (3mm). This gauge system is slowly being superseded by a metric diameter system. A 4 gauge screw's equivalent would therefore be metric 3. The second figure following the gauge number indicates the length of the screw, for example 4 x ¾in or 3 x 20mm.

The next indication on the packet will be the type of head that the screw has: slotted, Phillips or Posidriv, together with the shape of the head: countersunk or round. The screw may be made of a variety of metals: steel, either plain or plated; hardened steel, usually coated; or brass or japanned. It is no wonder, therefore, that we sometimes arrive home with the wrong type!

For this reason it makes a lot of sense to try and standardize wherever possible. Countersunk, plated screws in gauge sizes 4, 6, 8, and 10, in a selection of lengths, should suffice. In addition, the wheeled toys need gauge 10, slotted, round head brass screws in 1in and 2in lengths with washers. These screws do not appear to be sold in metric sizes.

CLEARANCE HOLES AND PILOT HOLES

When securing two pieces of wood with a woodscrew the top piece needs to be drilled with a hole equal to the diameter of the screw being used. This is referred to as the clearance hole and needs to be countersunk to take the screw head. The bottom piece of wood is drilled with a hole smaller than the clearance hole and this is called the pilot hole. The size of the pilot hole will vary slightly depending on the hardness of the wood, and some experimentation on a similar scrap of wood will soon determine the correct size. The screw should cut into the wood without too much effort but it must give a good grip. For example a gauge 4 screw (equivalent metric 3) would probably need a ¹⁄₁₆in (1.5mm) diameter pilot hole.

MOULDING PINS

Moulding pins with a diameter of ¹⁄₃₂in (1mm) and a length of ½in (12mm) are used mainly for holding rebated or butt joints in this book.

MAGNETS

Small magnets are extremely useful, when used in pairs, for holding doors shut, and they have many other uses. They are available round, rectangular, or in a strip to be cut as required. Glue magnets in position with epoxy resin, taking care to see that you have the right side uppermost!

— 6 —

Sanding

Sanding gets a whole chapter to itself in this book because it is so important. Toys need to be really smooth and splinter-free. The sanding stages need as much care and attention as the construction and design stages, and this is an area often skimped on because it is time-consuming and laborious.

The days have gone when you could go to the local ironmonger's for a sheet of 'sandpaper'! Abrasives are now very 'high-tech', and if you look at a catalogue of abrasive products the choice is enormous. For sanding wooden toys, aluminium oxide papers – which are tough, relatively inexpensive, and come in a wide range of grits – are the most suitable to use.

Two very useful machines to have in the workshop, which take away a lot of the drudgery, are the random orbital sander for flat surfaces and the disc sander for sanding edges and for shaping.

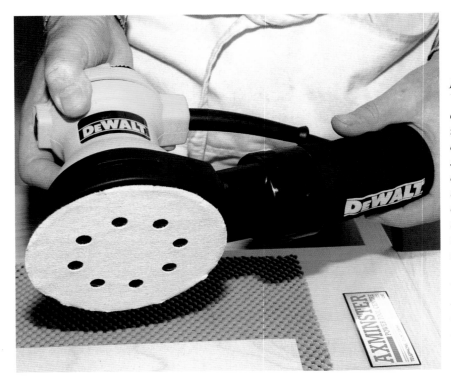

Fig.21 The De Walt random orbital sander with its built-in dust collection bag. The sanding discs have a Velcro back, and the holes allow the dust to be pulled up through the base of the machine into the collection bag. This machine has variable speed settings and can be operated with one hand, leaving the other hand free to hold the work.

THE RANDOM ORBITAL SANDER

This machine is hand-held and can be linked to a dust extractor, which will help to remove, at source, much of the dust produced. Some models have a built-in filter bag to collect the dust, and the sander we used during the manufacture of the toys in this book worked extremely well. The random orbit of the abrasive leaves a fine, virtually scratch-free finish.

The round, resin-coated aluminium oxide discs are attached to the base of the sander with a Velcro-type system, and the discs are perforated to enable the dust to be extracted. Discs from 40 to 240 grit are available. Even though birch plywood has a good finish it is advisable to orbital sand all the cut pieces prior to final assembly; in this way an excellent finish is obtained ready for painting and varnishing.

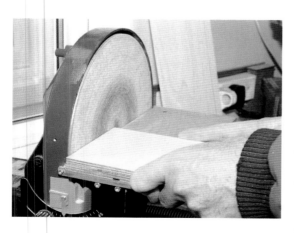

Fig.22 A 10in (250mm) diameter variable speed Proxxon disc sander. The gauge on the side indicates the table setting from 0 to 45 degrees. A vacuum extractor can be attached to remove the dust. The discs have a self-adhesive backing.

THE DISC SANDER

It is important to obtain really good, smooth edges to toys and for this task a disc sander is invaluable. The machine is also useful for shaping and rounding off edges quickly and efficiently. The table can be set at an angle and this makes it easy to form accurate mitre joints. Again much fine dust is created and the machine should be designed with a dust extraction point. The resin coated, aluminium oxide paper discs are usually self adhesive, and are available in a wide range of grits; 80 grit is a good all-round grit to use. The surface of the disc can be de-clogged from time to time with a rubber cleaning block sold especially for this purpose. If you have difficulty in removing an old disc try warming the surface first with a hair dryer to soften the adhesive.

SANDING FLAT SURFACES

Start sanding with 120 grit aluminium oxide using a random orbital sander, followed by 180 grit until all the scratches and tool marks are gone. Look at the wood obliquely in a good light to spot any imperfections. If all is satisfactory, sand with 220 grit. To raise the grain dampen the wood with a cloth and then allow it to dry for 10 to 20 minutes. Remove the fibres with large strokes using Webrax. With a fresh piece of 220 grit on the sander sand the surface again, repeat the grain-raising process, and then finally sand with 320 grit. By now the wood should feel as smooth as glass and is ready for staining, oiling or painting.

35

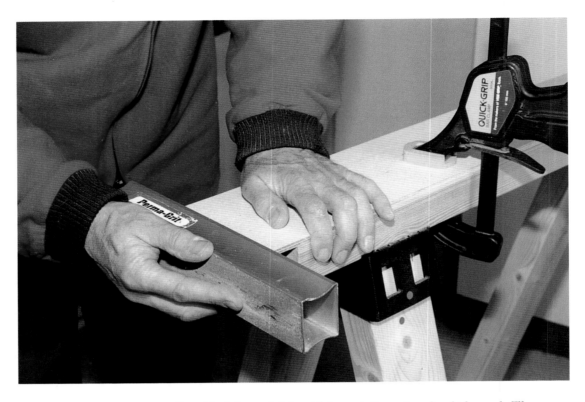

Fig.23 The Permagrit sanding block is useful for tidying up the cut ends of plywood. The author made the sawhorse using inexpensive, but very strong, brackets sold for this purpose and available from Craft Supplies. The sawhorse doubles up as a small bench and as a lathe stand. The advantage of making your own sawhorse is that it can be built to suit your personal height, thus eliminating unnecessary bending and back strain.

SANDING BY HAND

FLAT SURFACES

The abrasive needs to be applied flatly in order to maintain edges. When sanding by hand a foam or cork block that takes self-adhesive strips of resin-coated aluminium oxide abrasive is comfortable to hold and inexpensive. Grits of 80 to 400 are available; start with 80 and work up to 400 to obtain a good, smooth finish. Alternatively an aluminium sanding block, such as the Permagrit shown in Fig.23, with a permanent coating of tungsten carbide, is very efficient and will last for years. It is particularly useful for truing up the edges of cut ply.

SANDING SHAPES

Abrasive that is backed on to cloth, rather than on to paper, is flexible and comfortable to use and soft on the fingers. The abrasive can be bent or folded with no ill effect. It is usually sold on a roll, in different widths, and although it may seem expensive it can be washed out when it becomes clogged and reused, so it is economical in the long run. Again, this is available in a full range of grits from 80 to 400.

DRUM SANDERS
SANDING CURVES

For sanding inside and outside edges of circles, ovals, curves or abstract shapes a drum sander is ideal. The drums come in a range of diameters with a 12mm spindle to fit most power and bench drills, and will take 75mm wide cloth abrasive. These sanders are fast, accurate and safe. The manufacturers recommend spindle speeds of between 750 and 1,750rpm according to timber species. On small sections or expensive timbers, power sanding saves wood. Sawing a little

over the finished required size and sanding eliminates the need to plane. Start by using a coarse grit and then switch to finer grades until the finish is satisfactory.

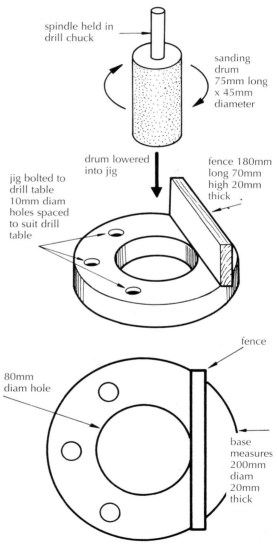

spindle held in drill chuck

sanding drum 75mm long x 45mm diameter

drum lowered into jig

fence 180mm long 70mm high 20mm thick

jig bolted to drill table 10mm diam holes spaced to suit drill table

fence

80mm diam hole

base measures 200mm diam 20mm thick

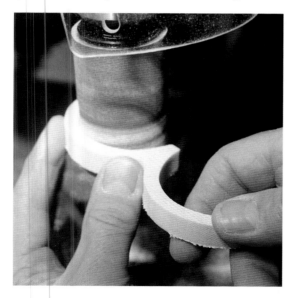

Fig.24 A Carroll drum sander mounted in a pillar drill and being used to sand an inside curve.

Fig.25 Home-made thicknessing jig.

Fig.26 The Carroll drum sander used with the home-made jig to thickness a strip of wood. The wood has been cross-hatched for clarity in the photograph. The dust extraction pipe is mounted behind the sander and takes away a good percentage of the dust.

THICKNESSING

A sanding drum, together with a home-made jig, can be used with a bench drill for thicknessing. The sanding drum is held in the machine and the wood passed between the fence on the jig and the sanding drum until the required thickness is arrived at. The drawing shows how you can make your own wooden thicknessing jig. The jig is designed to fit any size bench drill and the 10mm diameter holes can be spaced to suit a specific drill table. The distance between the outside of the drum and the fence is adjusted by swivelling the table. The hole in the centre enables the drum to be lowered slightly below the level of the jig. A great deal of dust is produced so a mask is essential, and the use of a dust extractor would also be sensible.

Do not press the work against the drum but rather let the abrasive do the work, and aim to remove only a small amount with each pass. Make sure that the piece of wood being put through the sander is at least 12in (300mm) long; short pieces are difficult to handle. It is vital that the permanently fitted fence is at right angles to the base.

ABRASIVES FOR WOODTURNING

CLOTH-BACKED ABRASIVE

An abrasive used for woodturning purposes must meet specific requirements: it must be flexible enough to get into all the curves and contours of the wood and it must also be possible to fold and twist it without any cracking or damage to the grain.

Hermes J-Flex 406, which is a cloth-backed aluminium oxide abrasive, is excellent for the woodturner. The cloth back makes it comfortable to hold as considerable heat is built-up during the sanding process. This product is sold in rolls of various widths and in grits from 80 to 400, and it can be washed and reused, which makes it economical.

NON-WOVEN WEB

A product such as Hermes Webrax is extremely useful. It consists of a mesh of nylon fibres onto which aluminium oxide or silicon carbide grains are firmly bonded by resin and resembles a pan scourer! As the grain is used up, fresh grain becomes exposed. The mesh is non-clogging and it can be washed out and re-used many times. Webrax is available in various forms, including hand pads and rolls. It is used by the woodturner for burnishing and de-burring and for applying polish. It is also excellent for de-

---

Tips for Sanding

- When woodturning always remove the toolrest and move away the tool-holder before starting to sand.
- Keep the cloth-backed abrasive moving all the time so that lines do not appear.
- Hold the abrasive under the work.
- Start with 40 grit and work through all the grits to get a good finish.
- Finish by burnishing the wood with Webrax.

nibbing between coats of paint when painting toys.

DUST

Dust is now looked upon as the woodworker's number one enemy in the workshop! Sanding with machinery does create a great deal of dust, which is both unpleasant for the operator and possibly harmful to the respiratory system.

Two lines of defence are recommended. The first is personal protection, and involves wearing a disposable mask or a respirator, or a turbo helmet. A suitable mask will be stamped with a European Standard; in the case of the disposable mask the standard is EN149 FFP 1 S or FFP 2 S. Do not be tempted by cheap, so-called 'nuisance masks', they do not meet this standard. The disposable mask is comfortable to wear and the type fitted with a valve, which directs the exhaled air downwards away from the eyes, is particularly suitable for spectacle wearers because it reduces the tendency of the lenses to fog-up with condensation. A disposable mask is designed to be worn for eight hours' constant use and is relatively inexpensive when compared with the respirator or the turbo helmet.

The second line of defence is to invest in a proper dust extractor, not that old vacuum cleaner banished long ago from the house! A good, efficient extractor should have a number of filters built in to remove the very fine particles of dust and prevent them from being re-circulated round the workshop. Some extractors are little more than just a method to suck up shavings. Dust extractors are intended to be attached to power tools by means of their hoses and should filter out a very high percentage of the dust. Although an extractor may not be a wildly exciting thing to buy, it will be money well spent. The filters do not last forever and need to be replaced from time to time as recommended by the manufacturer.

Fig.27 (Opposite) Safety: a disposable dust mask is essential even with a machine that has a dust collecting bag. The visor offers full-face and eye protection when sanding, grinding or woodturning. Ordinary prescription glasses do not offer enough protection on their own.

Construction Techniques

If the stages described here are accurately followed the result will be a strong, satisfactory toy. These are the methods that were used, where applicable, throughout this book.

CONSTRUCTING A PLYWOOD CARCASS USING A ROUTER

1. REBATING AND GROOVING PLYWOOD WITH A ROUTER

First set up the router in an accessory table and fit a ¼in diameter, parallel double-flute TCT cutter. This size of cutter is correct for ¼in plywood which is used throughout this book; you will need a 6mm cutter if your plywood is 6mm thick. Do not try to use a ¼in cutter for 6mm ply, or vice versa, as you will find that it will not work! The router will have some mechanism for fine adjustment of the depth of cut and the table will have a method of adjusting the position of the router from the fence. In this way the depth and the width can be set with extreme accuracy. It is always advisable to test the setting arrived at on a spare piece of plywood and make any necessary adjustments before starting to rout in earnest.

Pass the wood over the cutter and against the fence, keeping the fingers well

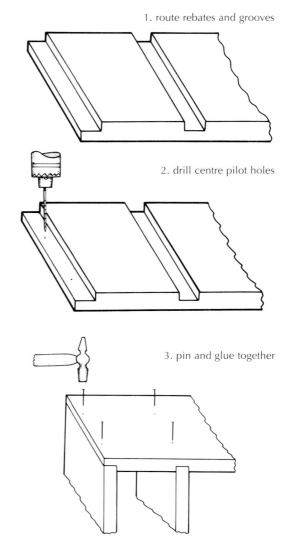

1. route rebates and grooves

2. drill centre pilot holes

3. pin and glue together

Fig.28 (Above & right) Rebating and grooving.

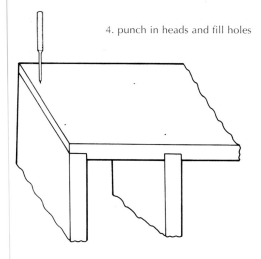

4. punch in heads and fill holes

away from the cutter and use a push stick for added safety. If the wood burns it is an indication that either the cutter is blunt or that the wood is being passed too slowly over the cutter. If the depth of cut required is more than that recommended in the instruction book for the router being used, it may be necessary to make several passes to achieve the desired cut. Rebates produced in this way will be accurate and the result will be a strong and lasting joint. A groove is cut in exactly the same way with the same cutter.

Alternatively, if you do not have a router table, grooves and rebates can be cut in the plunge mode, that is, with the router overhead; all routers are supplied with integral adjustable fences for this purpose. Remember that the wood being cut needs to be held firmly on the bench. We find that the router is quieter and safer to use in the inverted mode and for this reason we seldom remove it from its accessory table.

If you do not have a router to use then carcasses can be butt jointed and pinned quite satisfactorily. Minor adjustments will need to be made to the dimensions given,

and, as butt joints are not quite as strong as rebated ones, some reinforcement may be necessary.

2. DRILLING

A bench drill is ideal for the next stage, which involves drilling the pilot holes. The machine guarantees that the holes will be exactly at right angles. The drill should be fitted with a fine twist drill just slightly smaller than the diameter of the moulding pin that is going to be used. Drill along the centre of a rebate or a groove at intervals. The distance between the holes should be roughly about 2½in (64mm). Take care not to drill the holes at each end too near the edge to avoid splitting the wood.

If a bench drill is not available, a small mains drill can be used, but take care to hold the drill upright or, better still, use it in a drill stand.

3. SANDING

Sand along the rebates and grooves to remove any fine whiskers and sand all surfaces. Whiskers will be almost impossible to remove once the carcass is glued up.

4. GLUING AND PINNING

The purpose of pinning is to make it easier to assemble the carcass and to hold it together whilst the glue cures.

First carry out a dry run to make sure that the pieces to be joined fit together well; make any necessary adjustments. Once you are happy spread PVA adhesive along one rebate and press it to the

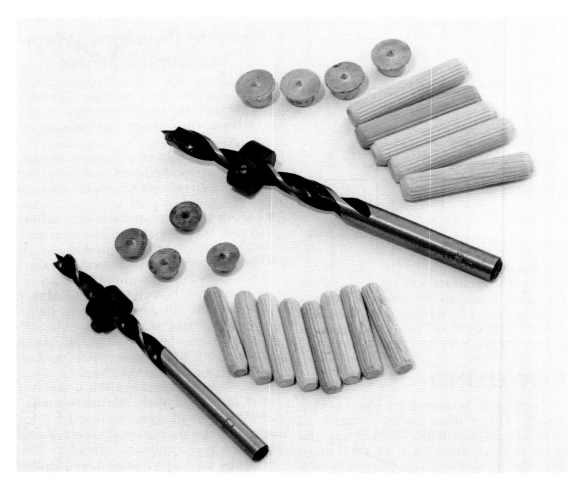

Fig.30 A typical dowelling set from Wolfcraft with 6 and 8mm diameter beechwood dowels, drills with adjustable depth stops and dowelling points.

dowel into the PVA instead. When the adhesive is dry, pare off the end of the dowel and sand smooth.

PROPRIETARY DOWELS AND DOWELLING SETS

Wooden dowels and dowelling points, together with matching lip and spur drills fitted with adjustable depth stops, are to be found separately or in combined sets in most woodworking retail outlets. These sets are not expensive, and we have used both the 6mm and 8mm sizes (metric only) for the cot project and for the table and chair project.

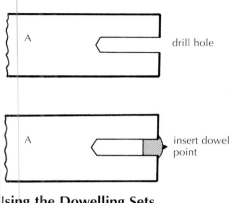

drill hole

insert dowel point

Using the Dowelling Sets

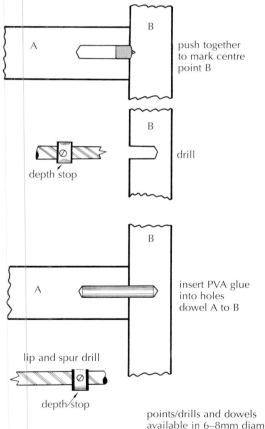

push together to mark centre point B

drill

depth stop

insert PVA glue into holes dowel A to B

lip and spur drill

depth stop

points/drills and dowels available in 6–8mm diam

Fig.31 Dowelling technique.

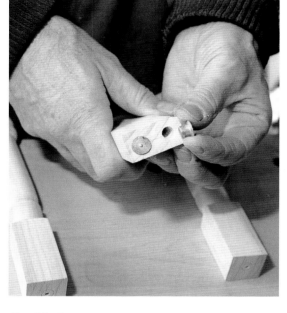

Fig.32 Inserting the dowel points into the pre-drilled holes.

The metal dowel points make accurate alignment and dowelling as simple as possible. The metal point is temporarily inserted into a hole drilled in the first piece of wood to the correct size and depth to match the dowel to be used. The point is then tapped against the wood to which it is to be joined so that a small indentation is made. This indicates where the second hole is to be drilled. Once the hole has been correctly drilled to the right diameter and depth the dowel is then glued into each hole and the two pieces of wood are tapped tightly together with a soft-faced hammer and a scrap of wood in order to protect the surface of the wood.

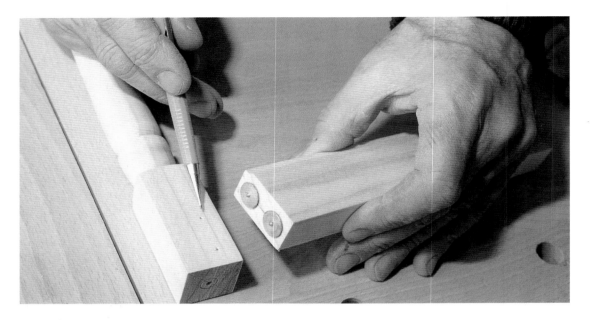

Fig.33 The pencil points to the indentations left by the dowel pins, which indicate where the holes are to be drilled for accurate alignment.

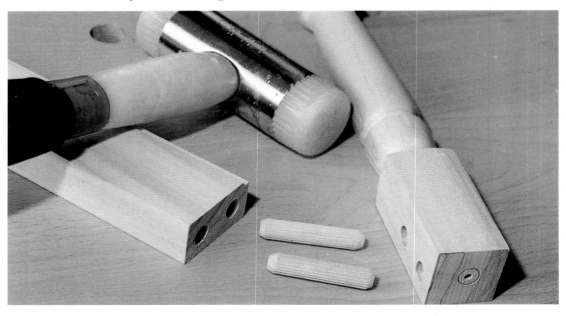

Fig.34 The leg and rail about to be glued and dowelled. The soft hammer can be used to tap the two pieces together without marking the wood.

— 8 —

Finishing

Children are naturally attracted to brightly coloured toys, but, as wood-workers, we tend to prefer as much of the wood as possible to remain natural. The toys do need some finish, however, or, over time, the wood will become dirty and lose its attraction.

The manufacturers of the products used in the book all state that their finishes are safe for children and conform with current toy-making standards.

OILS, PAINTS AND VARNISHES

FINISHING OILS

These are safe products that are easy to apply to the bare, sanded wood. They are practically odourless, free of unpleasant solvents and economical.

Apply the oil with a brush and wipe off any surplus immediately. Allow to dry

Fig.35 Liberon finishing oil, used in Project 3 to finish the traction engine's wheels.

according to the manufacturer's instructions before applying the next coat. Several coats will give a lustre to the natural wood whilst a freshening-up coat can be applied in the future if desired.

ACRYLIC PAINTS

There are now lots of acrylic craft paints to choose from, all available in a huge array of colours and brand names. They are inexpensive and easy to use and should be quite safe, but do check the label carefully first. This type of paint dries very quickly and brushes will wash out easily in water. Acrylic paints, because they are water-based, do tend to raise the wood grain, leaving a slightly rough texture to the wood.

ENAMEL PAINTS

If you want a bright, high-gloss finish you will need to use a gloss enamel paint certified safe for children's toys. Brushes will need to be cleaned in white spirit. There are plenty of colours to choose from in a selection of sizes, and some of the most popular colours are also available in spray cans.

VARNISHES

Varnishes suitable for toys come in matt, satin and gloss and are available in clear or in a wide range of colours. Apply two or three coats to the sanded wood with a good-quality brush, allowing two hours drying time between coats. If you are using acrylic varnishes the brushes are easily cleaned in water but other types will need

white spirit. Rub down between coats with fine abrasive before applying a coat of wax polish and buffing up with a cloth. Varnish can be applied over acrylic paintwork and lettering for protection against knocks and scrapes but do a test first on a scrap piece to make sure the colours do not weep and spoil your hard work!

BRUSHES

Do not economize on brushes. They are expensive and you will need several, so wash them out carefully after use, or clean them in white spirit, depending on the paint or varnish you have used. Nothing is more exasperating than constantly having to remove loose bristles from your brush or from the paintwork.

A wide, flat brush is good for covering large areas. Keep one such brush for paint, and a similar, but separate, brush for varnishing. Although you will want some small brushes for adding detail, use the largest size that will do the job.

TIPS FOR BETTER PAINTING

PREPARATION

The surfaces to be painted should be smooth and dust-free otherwise every blemish will show up. Use masking tape to mask off areas that are not to be painted.

STAGES

Try to think ahead. It is much easier to paint parts before assembly wherever this is possible. For example, paint wheels first

Fig. 36 Humbrol Super Enamel paints are available in a wide range of colours and are safe for toys.

Project 1 – Removal Lorry, Horsebox and Builder's Lorry

This is a design for a small four-wheeled lorry. The vehicle comprises a chassis and a cab, and construction involves the use of both the fretsaw and the lathe. There are plans and instructions to make three alternative bodies: a removal van (version A), a horsebox (version B) or a builder's lorry (version C). The chassis and the cab are the same in all three versions. In all cases the scale is roughly ½in. It is more

Fig.37 Builder's lorry.

Fig.38 Horsebox.

Fig.39 Removal lorry.

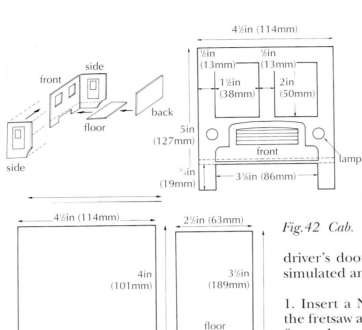

Fig.42 Cab.

THE CAB

The cab is constructed in ¼in (6mm) birch plywood with a hardwood offcut for the seat. The cab does not need its own roof because the overhang of the body forms a roof in the removal van and horsebox versions. This is an advantage during construction because it gives full access to the inside for fitting out and painting. A small rectangle of plywood forms the roof for the builder's lorry and this can be put in position once the inside is finished and painted. The doors are hinged with two small brass hinges on each door. Hinges are usually a weak area, and if the lorry is intended for a very young child you may decide not to have an opening door but just to simulate one. The photograph shows an opening

driver's door but the passenger's door is simulated and includes a side window.

1. Insert a No. 7 reversed-tooth blade in the fretsaw and cut out the five pieces that form the cab, following the dimensions given in Fig.42.
2. Mark out the doors and windows and drill the corners. Thread the blade through one of the drilled holes and cut out the windows and doors.
3. Sand all the edges carefully to remove any whiskers.
4. Butt joint the parts together by first gluing and pinning the side panels to the edges of the front panel, then fitting the floor and lastly the back, as illustrated in Fig.42.
5. Check that the cab fits correctly on the chassis but do not screw it in position at this stage.
6. Make a bench seat from hardwood to fit across the width of the cab. The height of the seat will depend upon the size of the figures you are planning to use.
7. Fret out a shape for the radiator from an offcut of ply and score the inner area with a sharp knife for the grille.

Fig.43 Cutting out the cab windows on the fretsaw on the passenger side.

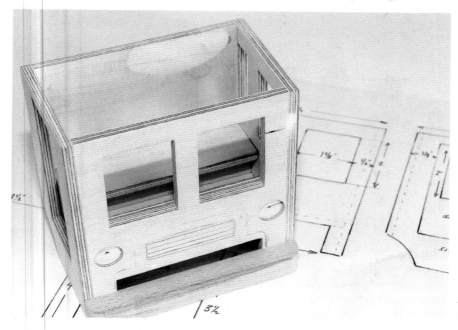

Fig.44 The assembled cab.

revolving centre. If the bolt is threaded right up to the head the drill chuck will not be able to grip it as firmly as a plain shank. Secure one nut on the shank end of the coach bolt with super glue. The length of the bolt very much depends on the work you wish to carry out.

Because the mandrel is supported at the tailstock end, a drill chuck fitted with a MT shank is not likely to work loose from the headstock; however, if the outside face of the wheel is to be shaped or decorated then it is an advantage if the drill chuck screws on to the headstock spindle so that it cannot work loose.

TURNING A BATCH OF WHEELS

1. Using a pair of compasses, draw out five wheel blanks each with a diameter of 2⅛in (54mm) on a thicknessed piece of ½in (12mm) hardwood. Fit a No. 9 blade in the fretsaw and cut out each of the blanks.
2. Drill each wheel with a ¼in (6mm) centre hole.
3. Mount the wheel mandrel in a drill chuck held in the headstock and fit a revolving centre in the tailstock. Thread the first blank onto the mandrel, tighten up the nut and bring up the tailstock. Using a spindle gouge, turn the blank to a diameter of 2in (50mm). This blank now forms the guide for the remainder of the wheels and stays in position on the mandrel. It has been painted bright red in the photographs for additional clarity.
4. Undo the nut, remove the washer and then mount the two blanks. Replace the washer and secure the nut. Bring up the tailstock to support the end of the

mandrel and turn the blanks until their diameters exactly match the completed guide wheel.
5. Mark a pencil line ⅜in (8mm) in from the edge of the face of the first wheel and make a V-cut with a beading tool to represent the tyre. Sand and burnish; remove the blank from the mandrel, reverse it and cut a tyre on the other side; sand and burnish. Remove the completed wheel and do the same for the second wheel.
6. Mount wheels three and four on the mandrel and repeat the process. Do not screw the wheels on to the chassis until they have been painted.

PETROL TANK, HEADLAMPS AND STEERING WHEEL

The steering wheel is purely decorative and it is not intended to move. Turn, or fret, a thin disc 1in (25mm) in diameter and glue it directly onto the dashboard, but check first that your chosen figure can sit behind the wheel comfortably!

Turn the petrol tank 2in (50mm) long x 1in (25mm) in diameter from a hardwood blank and then cut it in half. Glue one tank on either side of the chassis. Turn the head and tail lamps from small blanks of fine-grain hardwood.

MUDGUARDS

Cut the mudguards on the fretsaw from ¾in (19mm) thick hardwood. They are flat at the top to fit under the back container. You will need two for the back wheels and one cut in half for the front wheels. Sand

Fig.47 Sanding the inside curve of the mudguard on a Carroll drum sander mounted in a pillar drill. The chuck guard has been removed for clarity in the picture but should always be in position when drilling.

them well. Temporarily fit the wheels and the cab to the chassis to aid accurate positioning of the mudguards. You may need to sand the wheel arch slightly at the bottom of the cab so that the curve matches the mudguard. When you are happy, glue and cramp the mudguards into position.

PAINTING AND ASSEMBLY

1. Punch down all moulding pin heads and fill the holes with woodfiller.
2. Sand all surfaces thoroughly.
3. Apply several coats of finishing oil to the chassis with a brush, allowing plenty of drying time between each coat.

4. Paint the wheels. When they are dry screw them onto the chassis with No. 10 1in (25mm) round-headed brass screws, placing a washer between the wheel and the chassis.
5. Paint the inside and outside of the cab.
6. Fit the windscreen and steering wheel.
7. Secure the cab to the chassis by drilling a central countersunk hole through the floor and into the front chassis spacer. Insert a No. 6 ½in (12mm) woodscrew.
8. Now make a back for the lorry following the instructions for Version A, B or C and, when all the painting is complete, screw through the floor and into the chassis with two countersunk No.6 ½in (12mm) woodscrews.
9. Finally glue the roof into position for Version C.

Fig.48 Screwing on the wheels.

Fig.49 Painting the cab and door. It is easier to carry out this stage before the windows are glazed.

VERSION A – THE REMOVAL VAN

Our life in the Royal Air Force involved lots of moving about, and the removal van was quite a common sight outside the house. There was always the dread that not everything was going to fit in and it was a huge relief when the last bicycle was squeezed in and the ramp went up! If another child in the family has a doll's house then moving house can be played out, and the vehicle's size is roughly in keeping with ½in doll's house scale. The removal van is tough and attractive, and accessories, such as tea chests for packing up the books and china, can be made! The tailgate, which is hinged and drops down to form a ramp, is held shut with magnets.

1. Cut out the six pieces from the sheet of plywood with the dimensions shown in Fig.50. There are no windows in the sides of the removal van.

2. First do a dry run and check that the sides fit snugly against the back and top of

Materials

- 1 sheet of ¼in plywood 24 x 12in (600 x 300mm).
- Small sections of hardwood for the handle, the hinge support block, crossbeam and the ramp cross-treads.
- 2 small magnets.
- 1 x 1½in (40mm) long brass butt hinge with suitable brass screws.

65

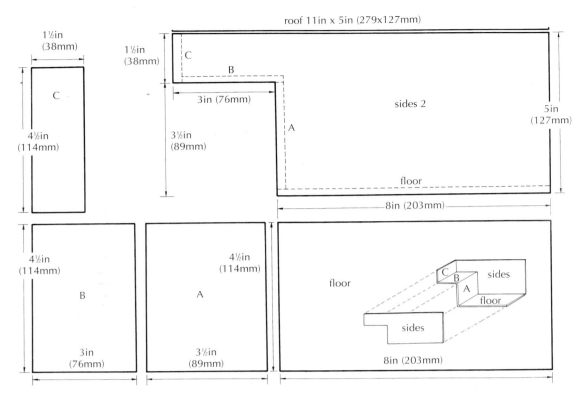

Fig.50 The removal van (version A) and the horsebox (version B).

the cab. Butt joint the sides to the floor and then join part A, part B and part C, in that order, to complete the box body.

3. Punch in the moulding pin heads and fill the holes; sand when dry.

4. Cut the roof – with measurements of 11 x 5in (279 x 127mm) – from plywood but do not glue and pin it in position at this stage. It will be easier, when all painting is complete, to screw the body to the chassis and then to put the roof on last.

5. To make the tailgate cut a rectangle from a piece of plywood with dimensions to fit inside the back of the container 4¾in high x 4¼in wide (120 x 114mm). Check the dimensions first before cutting to make sure that they are correct. Cut

grooves on the outside to simulate planking. Glue rows of thin hardwood strips at intervals across the width to act as treads on the inside of the ramp.

6. Cut a block of hardwood 1⅞ x ¾ x ½in (48 x 19 x 12mm) to fit between the chassis frames, and glue to the underside of the back edge as shown in Fig.52. This block provides a firm anchorage for the bottom hinge.

7. Glue a hardwood crossbeam 4½ x ½ x ¼in (114 x 12 x 6mm) widthwise across the underside of the roof to support the ramp when closed and to house the magnet.

8. Screw a 1½in (40mm) long brass butt hinge into position with one row of three holes in the plywood tailboard and the

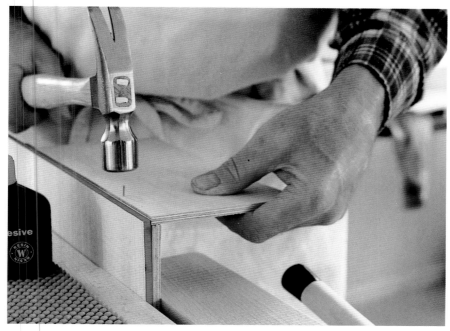

Fig.51 Pinning and gluing the body of the removal van. The scrap wood edged with red helps to line up the plywood accurately.

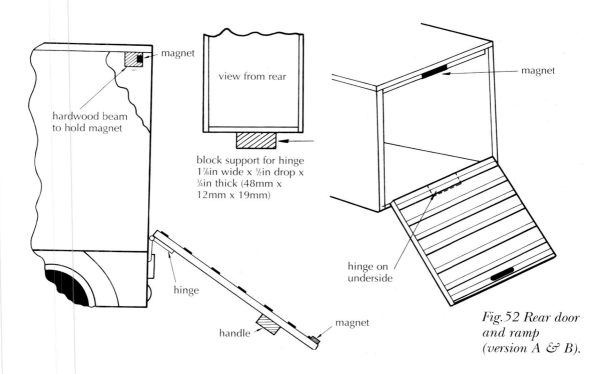

magnet

hardwood beam to hold magnet

view from rear

block support for hinge 1⅞in wide x ½in drop x ¾in thick (48mm x 12mm x 19mm)

magnet

hinge

hinge on underside

handle

magnet

Fig.52 Rear door and ramp (version A & B).

Fig.53 Gluing the hardwood crossbeam in position and cramping up with the Quick Grip bar cramp. The magnet is glued in the centre of the crossbeam.

Fig.54 Screwing the butt hinge to the tailboard.

Fig.55 Filing off the protruding screw points.

other 3 holes in the hardwood support block, using ½in No. 4 brass screws. The ends of the screws will protrude through the plywood, so file the points off until they are flush and smooth. Any hinge is a potentially weak point so chose a strong hinge and, for added strength, glue the screws into their holes with epoxy resin.

9. The tailboard is held closed by means of two magnets, one on the top inside edge of the tailboard and the other on the crossbeam under the roof; the magnets we used measured ⅞ x ¼ x ¼in (22 x 6 x 6mm). Chisel out a small rebate for each magnet and glue it in position with epoxy resin.

10. Cut a strip of hardwood 4½ x ½ x ¼in (114 x 12 x 6mm) and glue and cramp it in position two-thirds of the way up the tailboard to form a handle.

VERSION B – THE HORSEBOX

This is almost identical in design to the removal van but it is varnished rather than painted and has strips of wood for decoration. It also has high ventilation windows on each side. The horsebox can be played with in conjunction with the riding stable, which is included later in the book, and is in the same scale as the proprietary horses and riders selected for that project. Two horses can travel side by side and their riders can sit in the cab.

1. Follow the instructions for the removal van. The dimensions are the same, but note that both sides of the horsebox have

69

additional high ventilation windows, which need to be cut out using the fretsaw prior to assembly.

Materials

- 1 sheet of ¼in plywood 24 x 12in (600 x 300mm).
- Small sections of hardwood for the ramp handle, cross treads and hinge bar.
- Thin sections of hardwood for the wooden decoration on the container sides.
- 2 small magnets.
- 1 x 1½in (40mm) long brass butt hinge and brass screws.

---

2. The front interior area of the horsebox has a divider to separate the horses.

3. When the carcass has been glued and pinned together, you can decorate each side with thin strips of contrasting hardwood. Glue these strips onto the plywood and hold them firmly with cramps, or a heavy weight, until the adhesive is completely dry. In our example, the wood used was old mahogany thicknessed to ⅛in (3mm) with a sanding drum and cut into strips ⅜in (9mm) wide on the fretsaw. (*See* Chapter 6 which explains how to make a jig to use with a sanding drum to produce thicknessed wood.)

4. The ramp, on the inside, has rows of thin hardwood strips glued at intervals across its width to prevent the horses from slipping.

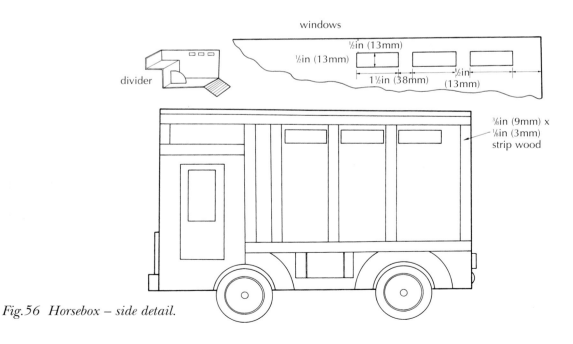

Fig.56 Horsebox – side detail.

Fig.57 Thicknessing mahogany strip for the horsebox with a home-made jig and sanding drum (see Chapter 6).

VERSION C – THE BUILDER'S LORRY

This is the simplest version of the lorry and provides a general-purpose pick-up lorry that can be filled with all manner of things, so is sure to give plenty of play value. You will need to add a roof to the cab for this version. There is plenty of scope for making lots of extras to go in the lorry, and a ladder, turned buckets and cones can be made.

1. Cut out the five pieces of plywood to form the lorry back and butt joint them together.
2. Cut a small piece of plywood 5 x 3in (127 x 76mm) to make the cab roof.
3. Take two sections of hardwood and form a ladder support with a crosspiece cut from a length of ¼in (6mm) dowel. Glue and pin the upright sections to the sides of the lorry.

4. To make the ladder cut two sections of hardwood 9 x ⅜ x ¼in (228 x 9 x 6mm) and sand them smooth. Tape both pieces firmly together with masking tape and drill ⅛in (3mm) holes at intervals of 1in (25mm); the drilled hole size should equal the diameter of the wooden skewer used to make the rungs. Place a piece of scrap wood underneath the wood whilst drilling to achieve a good clean hole.

Take some ⅛in (3mm) wooden barbecue skewers and cut nine 2in (50mm) lengths. Dip one end of each cut skewer into PVA and place it into the hole along one of the drilled ladder sides.

Materials

- 1 sheet of ¼in plywood 24 x 6in (600 x 150mm) for the lorry back.
- 1 piece of ¼in plywood 5 x 3 in (127 x 76mm) for the cab roof.
- Small strips of hardwood to make the ladder sides and the ladder support.
- ⅛in (3mm) diameter wooden barbecue skewers for the ladder rungs.
- Small offcuts of fine-grain hardwood for the turned buckets and cones.
- Short length of ¼in (6mm) dowel.

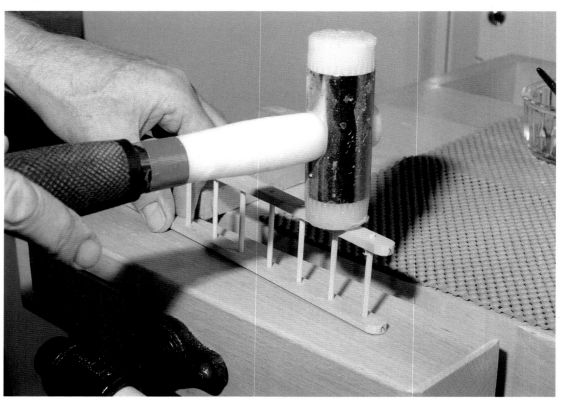

Fig.58 Putting the ladder together for the builder's lorry.

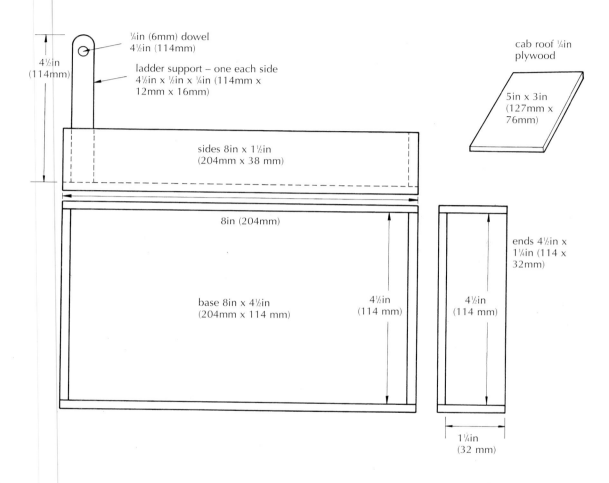

¼in (6mm) dowel
4½in (114mm)

ladder support – one each side
4½in x ½in x ⅝in (114mm x
12mm x 16mm)

4½in
(114mm)

cab roof ⅛in
plywood

5in x 3in
(127mm x
76mm)

sides 8in x 1½in
(204mm x 38 mm)

8in (204mm)

base 8in x 4½in
(204mm x 114 mm)

4½in
(114 mm)

4½in
(114 mm)

ends 4½in x
1¼in (114 x
32mm)

1¼in
(32 mm)

Fig.59 Builder's lorry.

When all nine rungs are in position line up the second ladder side, brush glue on the other ends of the rungs and locate them in the holes. Gently tap where necessary with a soft-faced hammer until the ladder is equally spaced along its distance. When the glue is set sand the edges well.

5. Turn some buckets and traffic cones and maybe an oil drum or two.

6. When all painting is complete screw the back to the chassis.

73

—10—

Project 2 – Farm

Fig.60 Farm.

The first toy our younger grandchildren want to have out, when they come to visit, is the farm. Some of the buildings and animals have stood the test of time well and originally belonged to our own children when they were young. The superb detail of today's tractors and farm implements, and the animals themselves, in metal and plastic, cannot really be improved on, and our efforts are concentrated on making the farm buildings. There is plenty of scope here and this farm design has been carefully thought out so that it is both a play arena for farm tractors, accessories and animals, and a storage box to keep them all together. To make it easy to put away, the farm can be lifted comfortably by an adult and stored in a cupboard or, because of its flat roof, it can be slid under a bed or stacked. Although the farm has been designed to suit Britain's farm animals and tractors, the height of the archways and the size of the pens can be adjusted for larger-scaled animals. The farm we made, illustrated in the photographs, was destined for our daughter-in-law's reception class at the primary school where she teaches, so it had to be tough! We would like to thank the Ertl Company for providing the Britain's farm animals and tractors for this project.

CUTTING LIST

The following pieces are cut from one sheet of ¼in birch plywood measuring 8 x 4ft (244 x 122cm).

Other Materials

- Moulding pins.
- No.4 1in (25mm) screws.
- PVA glue.
- Brick paper.
- Paints and varnish.

Part	Quantity	Material	Length (in/mm)	Width (in/mm)	Thickness (in/mm)
Front and back wall	2	Birch plywood	24/610	6/153	¼
Side walls	2	Birch plywood	18/458	6/153	¼
Internal wall	1	Birch plywood	18/458	5⅛/131	¼
Base	1	Birch plywood	23¾/603	18/458	¼
Doors	2	Birch plywood	10/254	5/127	¼
Centre lid	1	Birch plywood	17½/445	11⅜/290	¼
Left lid	1	Birch plywood	17½/445	6⅝/168	¼
Right lid	1	Birch plywood	17½/445	4⅝/117	¼
Beams	4	Hardwood	24/610	¾/19	¾/19
Beams	3	Hardwood	18/458	¾/19	¾/19

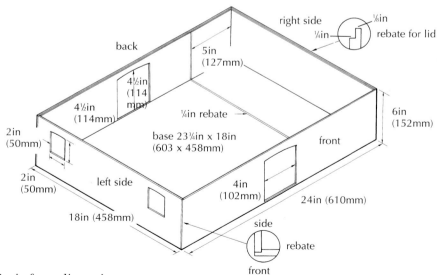

Fig.61 Basic farm dimensions.

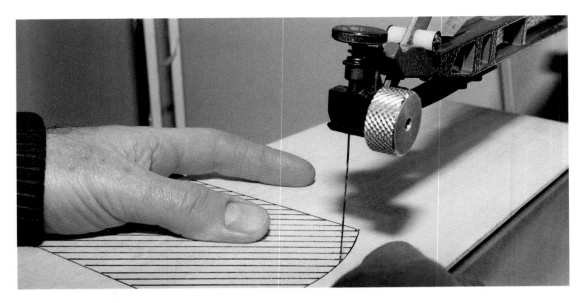

Fig.62 Cutting out the curved doorway for the farm entrance. The area to be removed has been cross-hatched for clarity.

Fig.63 It is worth the effort of sanding all the cut-out pieces of ply on both sides with a random orbital sander. The grey non-slip Wolfcraft mat will hold the ply whilst it is being sanded.

MAKING THE MAIN STRUCTURE

This is quite straightforward. Consult Chapter 7 for more detailed advice on carcass building. Where measurements are given for the thickness of the plywood you will notice that only the imperial measurement is given – the reasons for this are given in Chapter 5. The dimensions for the farm are shown in Fig.61 and the stages of construction are as follows:

1. Mark out the front, back and two side walls and cut out these four pieces.
2. Rout rebates, ¼in (6mm) wide and ⅛in (3mm) deep, along all four sides of the inside of the front and back walls.
3. Rout rebates, ¼in (6mm) wide and ⅛in (3mm) deep, along the inside top and bottom edges of the two side walls.
4. Rout a groove, ¼in (6mm) wide and ⅛in

Fig.64 The Veritas picture cramps are useful for holding a large carcass whilst the glue sets.

(3mm) deep, 5in (127mm) from the edge of the front and back walls.

5. Drill pilot holes with a 1/32in twist drill at intervals along the bottom and side rebates and the grooves. Do not drill holes along the top rebates.

6. Mark out the front and back arched doorways and the two windows on the left-hand side wall. Cut out these areas with a powered fretsaw.

7. Sand all the surfaces thoroughly with a random orbital sander or by hand.

8. Glue and pin the front, back and side walls together, cramp up and leave sufficient time for the glue to cure.

9. Mark and cut out the base, checking all measurements first. This will be especially important if you have used butt jointing as the method of joining the carcass instead of rebating. Rout a groove on the inside face of the base to match the grooves cut on the inside faces of the front and back walls. If you wish to give the impression of a flagstoned farmyard, mark out rectangles of slabs and score along the drawn lines with a sharp knife and a straight edge. Mind your fingers! Sand all the edges and then glue and pin the base in position.

10. Punch down all the moulding pin heads and fill the holes.

11. Mark and cut out the internal wall. Check that it slides down the prepared grooves but do not glue it in position yet; it will be easier to do the internal painting first. Note that the wall is lower than the external walls to allow space for the hardwood crossbeam that runs along its top.

12. Paint and varnish the inside of the construction now. Additional mock doors and windows, cut out from the plywood offcuts, can be painted and glued in position to give relief. You may wish to use

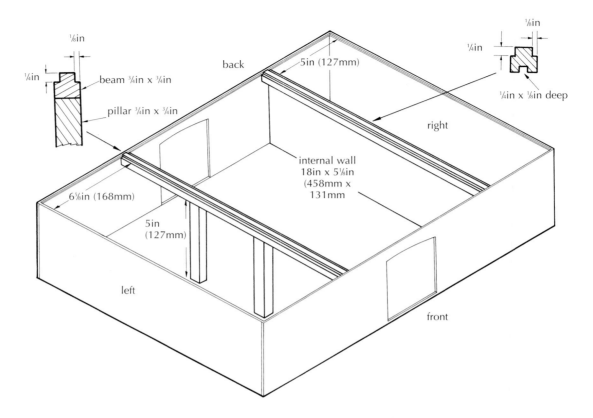

Fig.65 Arrangement of beams.

sheets of purchased brick or stone paper to decorate the walls, and these are best glued on with wallpaper paste.

CONSTRUCTING THE BEAMS

There are two hardwood beams fitted across the carcass. The left-hand one is supported by two upright beams to form a barn area. The right-hand beam has a groove running along its length on the underside and locates on top of the solid internal wall. The beams are screwed in very securely because they may well be used as a method of lifting the farm when the lids are off. Fig.65 shows the positions of the beams.

1. Prepare three lengths of hardwood ¾ x ¾ x 18in (19 x 19 x 458mm) to represent oak beams.

2. Take two lengths and rebate them along both top edges, ¼in (6mm) deep and ⅛in (3mm) wide. These are the beams that run from front to back across the carcass and the rebates on the top edges form a lip to support the lids.

3. Take one of the rebated beams and rout a groove ¼in (6mm) wide, ⅛in (3mm) deep down the centre of the underside. This is the beam that sits on top of the internal

Fig.66 Check that the beams fit together correctly before staining them.

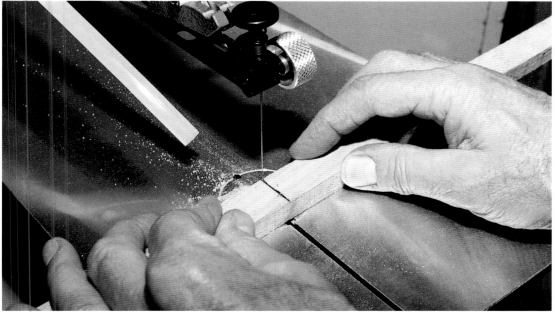

Fig.67 Cutting the hardwood beams to length on the Hegner. A saw like this will easily cut up to 2in (50mm). Note the plastic pipe on the left of the blade, which is used to blow the dust away from the cutting line, or, when the machine is connected to a vacuum extractor, will collect up to 98 per cent of the dust.

1. Take one length of beam 24 x ¾ x ¾in (610 x 19 x 19mm) and bandsaw it down the centre.

2. Round off the square ends on a sander.

3. Once all the decorating is finished, position each length along the top of the front and back, over the doorway, and glue and cramp it in position. As well as acting as handles for lifting the farm these beams will cover the screw holes.

PAINTING AND DETAILING THE EXTERIOR

The exterior detailing and painting will give you an opportunity to display your artistic skills to the full, and the results can be as plain or as elaborate as you wish! Mask off a top strip along the front and back where the hardwood handles are to be glued and any area where you intend to position additional mock doors or windows or the farm's name-board, and leave these areas unpainted.

Apply a primer and a base coat first and then paint on any details. We gave the inside of the right hand storage area several coats of varnish because we felt it was more likely to get scratched and scraped. Extra mock doors and windows can be cut from offcuts of ply and suitably painted and detailed before being glued in position with contact adhesive on non-painted areas.

ACCESSORIES

There will be plenty of offcuts of plywood left over and these can be used to make small pens, a pig sty, a stable, chicken house and so on. A plan for a pen is shown in Fig.69.

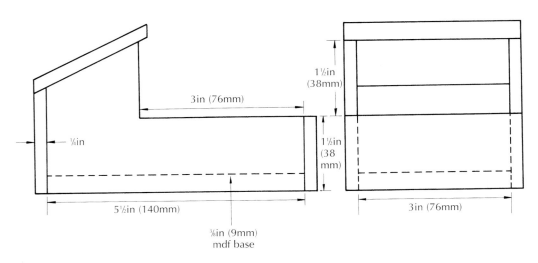

3in (76mm)

¼in

5½in (140mm)

⅜in (9mm) mdf base

1½in (38mm)

1½in (38 mm)

3in (76mm)

Fig.69 Animal pen.

Fig. 70 Mock doors and windows can be cut out from scraps of plywood and glued with a contact adhesive such as Copydex to add relief.

Fig. 71 The side of the farm showing paintwork and brick paper inserts. The Britain's tractors and farm animals were kindly donated by the Ertl Company.

Fig.72 A small animal pen.

PENS

The pens shown are cut out on the fretsaw, sanded and butt jointed and pinned on to a thicker MDF base. This is an example where an offcut of MDF comes in handy! The walls are then scored to resemble brickwork and the roof to represent tiles.

HEDGES

Fences, hedges and gates are useful so that the child can form fields to put the animals in, but they are subject to damage from a careless foot! It is best to keep them as simple as possible, and do make sure they stand upright on carpet, as it is most frustrating if they keep falling over.

NAME-BOARD

Finally the farm must have a name! Cut out a suitable piece of plywood and write the chosen name on by hand or, for a more professional look, use transfer rub-off letters. Alternatively you may consider designing something suitable on a computer and printing it out on card, which can then be glued to the name-board.

Project 3 – Traction Engine

This is a robust, good-looking toy, which is suitable for most young children. It is fun to turn and will not cost very much in materials if you have a selection of offcuts to use up. Two turned figures sit in the driving cab. It must be remembered that

this is not a model; there is always a temptation to add more sophisticated detail – the pistons, for example, could move in and out – but small moving parts are very susceptible to damage. All spigots are firmly glued into holes throughout

Fig. 73 Traction engine.

and no nails are used. The use of different-coloured woods makes this traction engine a very attractive toy; the bare, sanded wood is left unpainted, several coats of finishing oil being applied instead to impart a pleasing, natural lustre.

WOOD

The first thing to do is to prepare the blanks tabulated in the cutting list. Try to choose a variety of hardwoods whose colours contrast well. Sycamore, walnut, holly, hornbeam, box, amarillo, lemon-wood and ebony were all used in our example. Bring the wood you are going

Other Materials

- Epoxy resin adhesive.
- 6 No. 10 round-headed screws, 2in (50mm) long.

Woodturning Equipment Used

- Small Woodturning Lathe.
- Combination chuck with standard and small set of jaws.
- Indexing facility on either the lathe or the chuck.
- Ian Wilkie stepped friction drive.
- Screw chuck.

CUTTING LIST

Part	Quantity	Diameter (in/mm)	Length (in/mm)	Width (in/mm)	Thickness (in/mm)
Large wheels	2	4/100			1⅜/35
Small wheels	2	3/75			1/25
Flywheel	1	3/75			¾/20
Body	1		5⅛/130	2⅜in/60	2¾/70
Boiler	1		5¾/145	2/50	2/50
Smokebox	1		2/50	2/50	2/50
Smokebox cover	1	2/50			1/25
Smokestack	1		2/50	1¼/30	1¼/30
			5⅛/130	1¼in/30	1¼/30
Piston and cylinder	1		2⅜/60	1/25	1/25
Base	1		2¼/55	1/25	½/12
Engine block	1		2⅜/60	¾/20	¾/20
Pillars (pen blank size)	4		6/150	½/12	½/12
Canopy	1		5½/140	2¾/70	⅜/10
Canopy edging	2		5½/140	⅝/15	¼/6
	2		2¾/70	⅝/15	¼/6
Front wheel assembly	1	2/50			½/12
Axle	1		3⅛/80	¾/20	¾/20
Optional extras	an assortment of small blanks				

overall length 12½in, height 9¼in, width 4¾in (320mm x 235mm x 120mm)

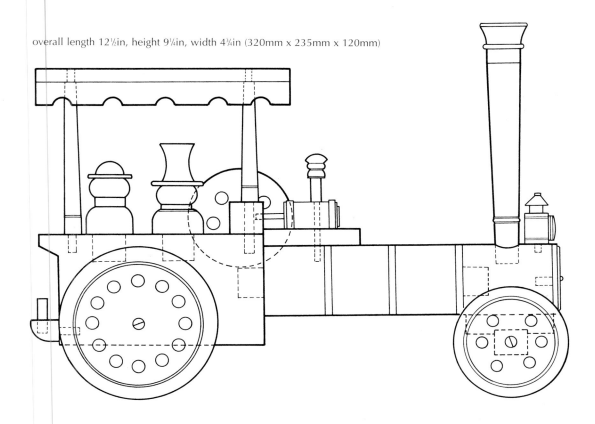

Fig. 74   Turned toy traction engine.

Fig. 75   The contrasting woods prepared for the traction engine project.

to use into the workshop, preferably some weeks before you are going to use it. This allows the timber time to 'settle', and any cracks, warping and other defects will become noticeable and the wood can be discarded.

THE WHEELS

The two back wheels are larger than the front but all four are turned and drilled in a similar way. The large wheels are decorated, and this is where the indexing facility on the lathe or the chuck comes into use. If you do not have indexing then

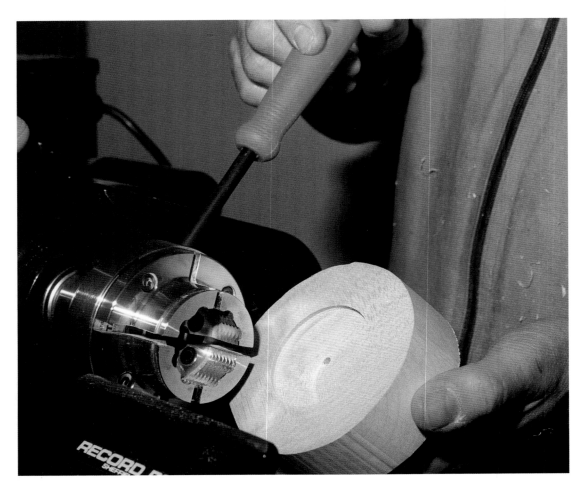

Fig. 76 The Junior Bulldog jaws for the Multistar Titan chuck about to be expanded into the prepared dovetail recess.

I suggest that you decorate your wheels in an alternative way. The flywheel is the same diameter as the front wheels but is not as thick.

1. Mount the wheel blank on a screw chuck held in the headstock, and turn to the round with a spindle gouge until the surface is smooth and the diameter is reduced to 3¾in (95mm) for the large wheels and 2¾in (70mm) for the smaller wheels. Face off the front surface of the blank and cut a dovetail to suit the chuck jaws, in expansion mode, which you intend to use. Use the standard jaws for the large wheels and the smaller jaws for the small wheels.

2. Replace the screw chuck with an indexed combination chuck, remove the blank from the screw chuck and expand

Fig. 77 Drilling the holes round the face of the wheel. Note the index bar being used to lock the chuck at each position and the Multistar drilling guide, which ensures that the holes are drilled accurately.

the chuck jaws into the prepared dovetail recess. Face off the surface to give a thickness of 1⅛in (30mm) for the large wheels and ¾in (20mm) for the small wheels. Cut a decorative V with a spindle gouge ⅜in (10mm) in from the edge.

3. Position an index bar to use with the indexed chuck or use the built-in indexing if your lathe has it.

4. Drill a ring of twelve holes round the large wheels; to do this you will need to set up a drilling jig. Set the depth stop so that the hole is only drilled ½in (12mm) into the wood, not right through. There are special drilling and boring jigs for this purpose. Place the index pin in a hole in the chuck and drill the first hole with a ¼in (6mm) diameter drill bit; rotate the chuck by hand to the next but one hole, put the index pin in position and drill the next hole. Cont-

inue in this way using every other index hole until twelve holes have been drilled. For the small wheels drill six equally spaced holes to a depth of ⅜in (8mm) using every fourth index hole. If your hole is 'ragged' you are probably drilling too slowly or you have a blunt drill bit.

5. The flywheel is turned in exactly the same way as the small front wheels, but the wheel thickness is ⅝in (15mm) and the eight holes are drilled right through. Choose some other method of decoration if no indexing facility is available.

THE BODY

This is not turned but is made from one block of wood 5¼ x 2⅜ x 2¾in (130 x 60 x 70mm) thick.

1. Sand all the surfaces carefully, using a disc sander if you have one.
2. Cut out a shape at the back as shown in Fig.74.
3. Drill one hole ¾in (19mm) at one end so that the top of the boiler will come just below the top surface of the body

Fig. 78 Turning the driver.

(Fig.79). Drill a further two staggered holes ¾ x ⅝in (19 x15mm) deep in the top surface to take the driver and his mate.

4. Turn the driver and mate with ¾ x ⅝in (19 x 15mm) long spigots to seat well down into the drilled holes .

THE BOILER AND SMOKEBOX

1. Select two strongly contrasting woods for the boiler and smokebox (we used hornbeam and dark walnut). Mount a ring centre in the headstock and a revolving centre in the tailstock. The ring centre will make it easy to remount the work accurately.

2. Turn the boiler between centres to make a cylinder measuring 5¾ x 2in (145 x 50mm) in diameter, and cut two rings for decoration. With a parting tool cut a spigot at each end ¾in in diameter x ⅝in long (19 x 15mm). Sand and burnish and remove from the lathe.

3. Take a blank 2 x 2 x 2in (50 x 50 x 50mm) for the smokebox and drill a ¾in (19mm) hole at the centre of one end, ⅝in (15mm) deep, and centre-pop the other end. Glue the boiler with the spigot into the corresponding smokebox hole and bring up the tailstock to act as a cramp.

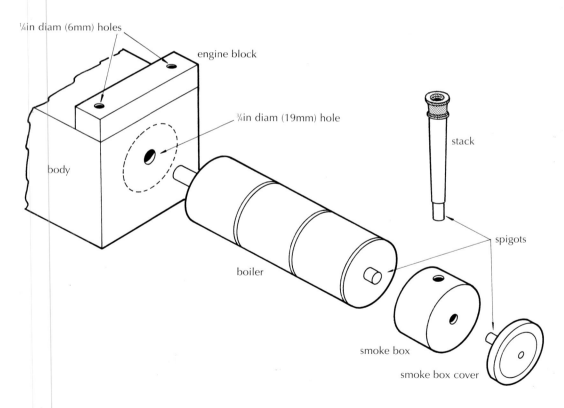

Fig. 79 Boiler, smokebox and stack.

4. When the glue is dry turn the smoke-box to the round to match the diameter of the boiler. True up the outer end of the smokebox with a parting tool and make the final cut with the long point of an oval skew, leaving a waste spigot to part off.

5. Sand and burnish.

6. Glue the boiler and the body together with epoxy resin.

SMOKEBOX COVER

1. Cut a blank of fine grain wood 2in diameter by 1in thick (50 x 25mm) and hot-melt glue it to a glue chuck mounted on a screw chuck.

2. Turn the blank to the round to 1¾in (45mm) diameter.

3. Face off the outer end and shape,

Fig.80 The boiler and smokebox held between centres on the lathe whilst the glue cures. A Record CL5 lathe was used for this project.

Fig.81 Turning the smokebox cover.

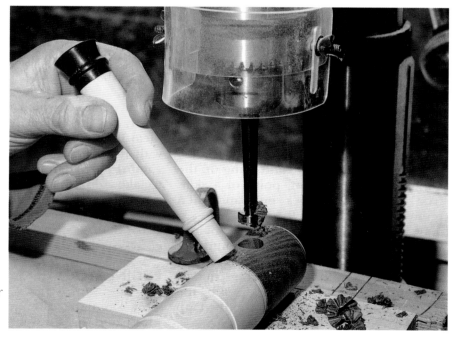

Fig.82 Drilling the top of the smokebox with a saw-tooth Forstner bit to take the smokestack.

93

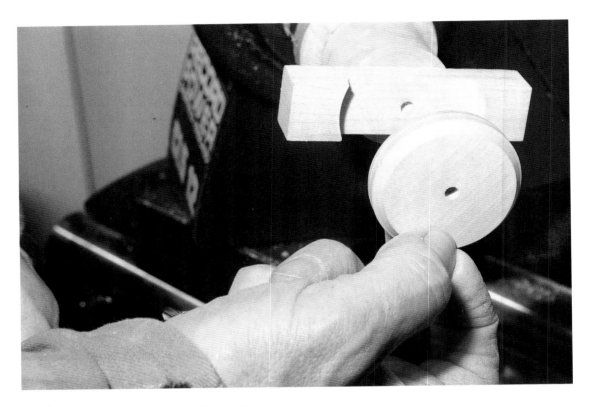

Fig.87 Turning the cross-axle for the front wheel assembly.

Optional Extras

● A tow hook, a bucket, lamps and a whistle can all be fabricated from small offcuts if required.

smokestack. Add the lamp and the rear hook if these have been turned.

3. Apply two coats of finishing oil to the part-assembled traction engine, the two figures and all the wheels.

4. Fix the wheels to the cross-axle and screw the whole assembly up through the cross-axle into the smokebox as shown in Fig. 86.

5. Place the toy on a flat surface and use some scraps of wood to lift up the rear of the body so that it is horizontal. Check with a square to see that the vertical edge of the body is true.

6. With a home-made scriber block and a marking gauge mark the position of the pilot holes for the rear wheels on each side of the body. Do not hurry this stage! Centre-pop, drill the pilot holes for the screws and then screw on the wheels, making sure that they rotate freely; you can use washers if you think it is necessary.

7. Fit the flywheel to the left-hand side of the engine block so that it can also rotate.

8. Pop the driver and his mate into their holes, steam up, and away you go!

98

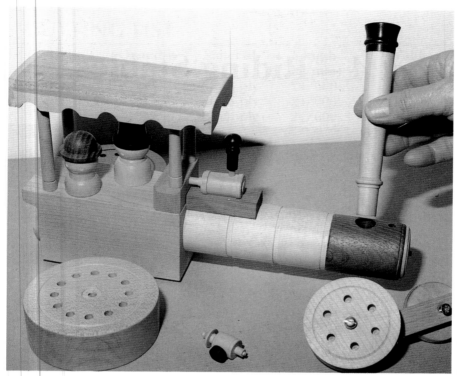

Fig.88 Gluing in the smokestack.

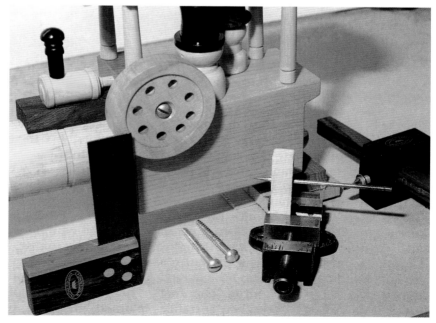

Fig.89 Marking the position for the wheels.

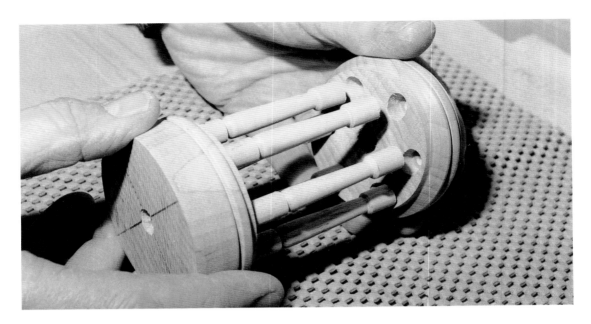

Fig. 96 Fitting the cupola together. Carry out a dry run before finally gluing up.

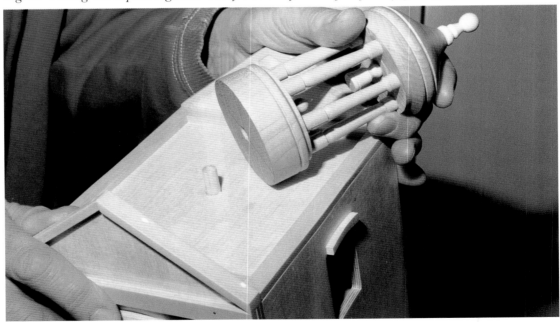

Fig. 97 The completed, but unpainted, cupola with its bell in position about to be located on a dowel on the roof of the tower.

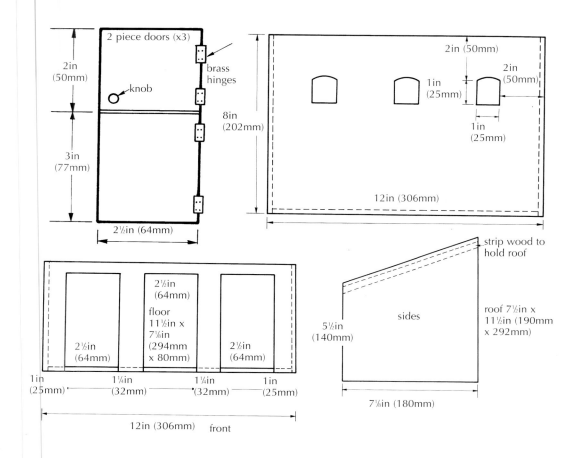

Fig.98 The stables.

8. Turn a small rounded finial to place on top of the cupola for the final touch.
9. Drill a ⅜in (9mm) hole in the roof of the carcass. Glue one end of a short dowel into the hole and locate the other end in the base of the tower to hold it in position.

THE STABLE BLOCK AND THE TACK ROOM

The stable has three stalls with top and bottom opening doors and three high windows with bars. The tack room has a double opening door and two barred windows. The two buildings have the same overall measurements.

1. Sand two sheets of plywood 24 x 24in (600 x 600mm) thoroughly with an orbital sander and then mark out the fourteen pieces that make up the stable and tack room, taking the measurements from Figs.98 and 99.
2. Cut out the pieces with the fretsaw. First drill the corners of the doors and windows

107

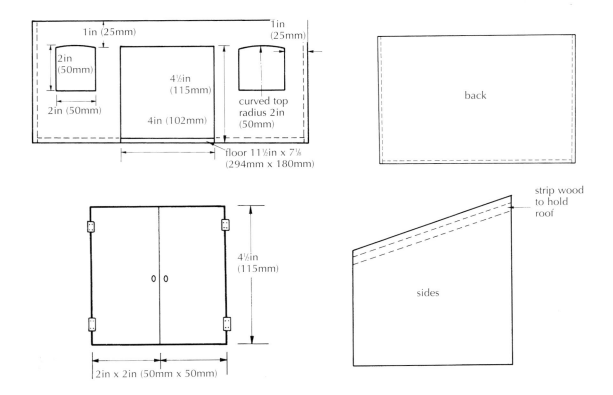

1in (25mm)

1in (25mm)

2in (50mm)

4½in (115mm)

2in (50mm)

4in (102mm)

curved top radius 2in (50mm)

floor 11½in x 7⅛ (294mm x 180mm)

back

strip wood to hold roof

4½in (115mm)

0 0

sides

2in x 2in (50mm x 50mm)

Fig.99 Tack room.

and then cut them out. Keep the cut-out pieces carefully because they will be needed later to form doors.

3. Drill pilot holes as follows:
● along the edges of the front and back where the side walls butt-on.
● along the bottom edges of the front, back and sides where the floor will be butted in.
● for the stable block alone: along the two positions, front and back, where the internal divisions for the horse stalls are to be fitted.

4. Tidy up the cut edges and the drilled holes with a sander if necessary.

5. Now assemble the pieces together in the following sequence to form the two separate buildings:
● glue and pin the front to the two sides.
● next put in the floor.
● then the back.
● lastly, for the stable, the two stall dividers. Leave the roofs at this stage.

6. Cut four lengths of strip hardwood and glue them ¼in (6mm) down from the top inside face of the sides to form a ledge for the drop-in roofs to rest on. Trim and sand the edges of the roof pieces so that they fit snugly.

7. Cut two lengths of hardwood 12 x 1 x ⅛in (300 x 25 x 3mm) thick to form bargeboards. Glue them along the front

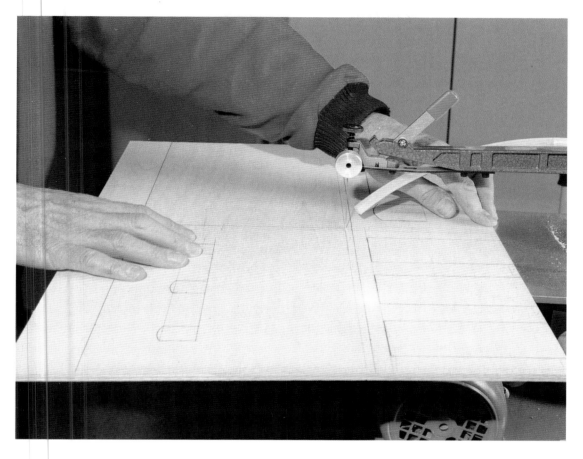

Fig.100 Cutting out the pieces for the stables using the Hegner fretsaw. The blower keeps the dust well clear of the marked cutting line.

of each building; they are a little higher than the roof and will disguise the plywood endgrain.

8. Glue a strip of wood down the left-hand side of each of the three stable doorways to form a door frame.

FOR THE STABLE ONLY

1. Make three frames slightly larger than the high windows at the back of the stalls (Figs. 101, 102, 105).

2. Drill the top and bottom of each frame and insert thin dowels into the holes to represent bars. Wooden barbecue skewers are a good source of thin dowel.

3. Take the three cut-out door pieces for the stable and trim the top third off in each case to form the upper stable door.

4. When the building and the doors have been painted, fit two small hinges to each door and glue them in position with epoxy resin before tapping in small brass nails. These very small hinges should come with brass nails of the correct

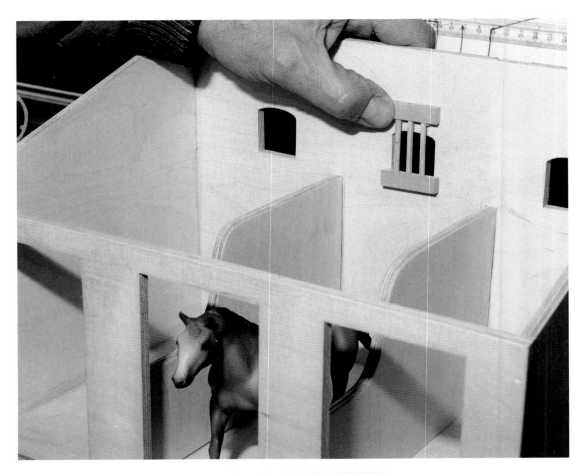

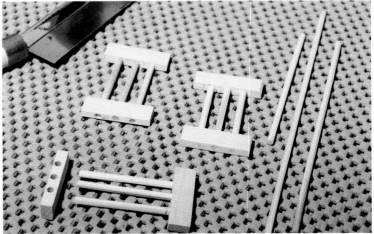

Fig.101 Checking that the windows are the correct size and that the horse likes his stable! Note the divisions between the stalls – these are optional.

Fig.102 Making up the barred windows for the stable block from strip wood and wooden barbecue skewers.

Fig.103 Completed view of the stable block. The horses and riders were purchased from W. Hobby Ltd.

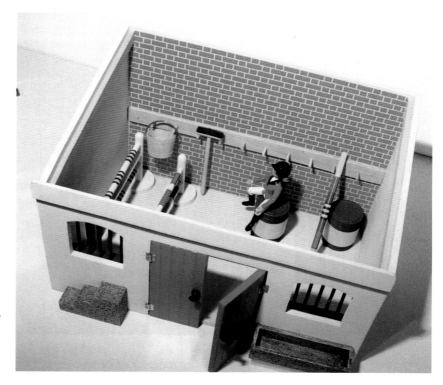

Fig.104 The completed view of the tack room with some of the extra accessories.

Fig.122 *Shaping the underside of the body of the twirler top with a spindle gouge.*

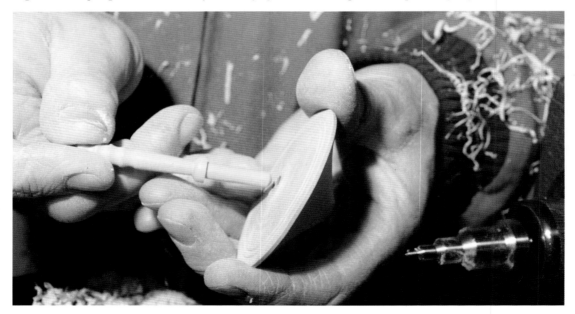

Fig.123 *Fitting the turned stem to the body.*

128

5. Shape the top end of the stem and then the lower end. Move the tailstock out of the way and finish shaping the spinning point.
6. Gently sand, burnish and polish, taking care not to polish the spigot.
7. Finally part off with a skew chisel at the headstock end.
8. Glue the spigot into the body and you are ready for your first twirl!

TWO GAMES TO PLAY WITH TWIRLERS

In the first game, all the players have an equal number of twirlers, and at a given signal they start their pieces spinning. The first player to have all their twirlers spinning simultaneously is the winner.

Note that if a piece falls over it may be picked up and restarted.

In the second game a player starts the twirler spinning and then has to undertake an agreed task before the twirler falls over – for instance he or she may have to run three times round the apple tree or tie up a shoelace!

THE SIX-SIDED TEETOTUM

The teetotum illustrated in Fig.124 is a twirler that can be used to make completely random decisions for games

blank 3¾in x 1½in (95mm x 38mm)square

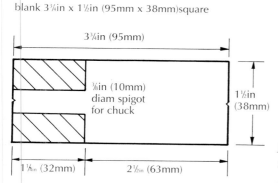

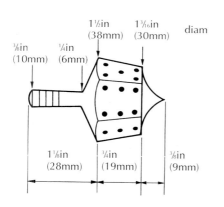

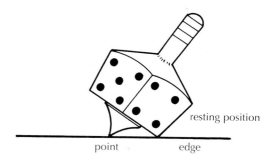

Fig.124 (Above and bottom left) Six-sided teetotum.

Fig.125. Marking out the position of the flats, which will be formed with a small block plane.

129

Fig.126 Engraving the recessed dots on each flat with a round burr held in a flexible drive. Note that the headstock spindle is locked for this operation.

of chance, in the same manner as dice. As the top ceases to rotate it starts to wobble and eventually falls to rest to show a score, mark or colour. The teetotum in the photograph is turned from one blank of hardwood.

1. Cut a blank of hardwood 3¾in long x 1½ x 1½in (95 x 38 x 38mm) and centre-pop each end. Choose a light-coloured wood so that the dots will show up well.
2. Mount the blank between centres with a ring centre in the headstock and a revolving centre in the tailstock, and turn it to a diameter of 1½in (38mm).
3. Form a spigot at one end 1¼in long and ⅜in in diameter (32 x 8mm), and then remove the wood from the lathe.
4. Screw a combination chuck to the headstock, fitted with small jaws to hold

the turned spigot on the blank, and bring up tailstock support.
5. Mark off a line 1¼in (32mm) from the tailstock end and turn a conical shape for the body as shown in the drawing.
6. Partly form the pointed base and the upper area of the body.
7. Stop the lathe and position the toolrest parallel to the tapered body. Use the index facility of the lathe if it has one, or alternatively use an indexed chuck and a bar, and mark six equal divisions around the circumference of the partly turned teetotum with a pencil. Make sure that the lathe is not switched on whilst the index pin is still engaged! It is wisest to pull out the plug completely.
8. With a small, sharp block plane form the six flats between the marked lines. Finish off with a hand sanding block. It

is important that the lower edges of the flats are at right angles to the axis, otherwise the top will not settle positively when it comes to rest, causing no end of heated arguments between the players!

9. You can decorate each facet in a number of ways, and it is easiest to do this whilst the top is still held in the lathe. Each flat can be painted a different colour, which will help very young children with their colour recognition. Another possibility is to apply instant transfer letters or numbers directly on to the wood. Those woodworkers with a pyrography iron could consider burning

marks into the wood. We have opted for recessed dots on each facet, like those on a dice, and these have been made using a small circular burr mounted in a flexible shaft which in turn is powered by a small drill or router. On a dice the two opposite sides always total seven, so this is what we have done with the teetotum. Once the indentations have been made they can be filled with paint or coloured with a pen to show up clearly. Any paint overspill can be carefully sanded away when dry.

10. Now form the spinning point but round it off slightly by gentle sanding. Complete the stem end and part off the top with the long point of a skew.

Fig.127 The recessed dots can be painted with acrylic colour. When the paint is thoroughly dry sand off the surface to give a crisp edge to each dot.

131

that it is the uppermost character that appears when the top comes to rest that decides the play.

THE YO-YO

This toy has been around since the 18th century and has been in and out of fashion over the years. Recently there has been something of a resurgence of interest in the school playground as the yo-yo has appeared for another airing; now there are geared plastic models, which can do all sorts of tricks! However, a wooden yo-yo is a fun item to turn, and it can be made and personalized for a particular child, which makes it just a little more special.

In this project two methods of construction are described and illustrated. The first needs very little equipment and the yo-yo is turned in one piece. The second utilizes a combination chuck and involves more precise turning. The finished yo-yos weigh just under 2oz apiece, and the weight does seem to be important when it comes to operating them. The special twisted strings can be purchased in packs from a toyshop.

YO-YO TURNED BETWEEN CENTRES

This is the simplest method, and does not involve using expensive equipment. Any type of ring centre and revolving centre will be quite adequate. The drawing with dimensions is shown in Fig.129.

1. Prepare a blank 2¾ x 2¾ x 1½in (70 x 70 x 40mm) thick, from dense wood to give sufficient weight to the yo-yo. Mark the centres on both faces and centre-pop. Cut off the corners and mount the blank between centres with a ring centre in the headstock and a revolving centre in the tailstock.

2. With the lathe set to 2,000rpm turn the blank to a diameter of 2⅜in (60mm), using a roughing-out gouge.

3. Mark the centre line accurately. The lathe must be stationary whilst this is being done. Draw lines 1/16in (2mm) either side of the centre line, and with a thin parting tool start to cut the slot down to 5/16in (8mm). It is important to cut a parallel-sided slot and to avoid widening it out any further.

4. Start to shape the outboard side of the blank with a 5/16in (8mm) spindle gouge.

5. Reverse the work and turn the other side to match. Use a thin parting tool to turn right up to the drive.

6. Cut a slight chamfer each side of the slot with a spindle gouge.

7. Remove the toolrest and sand the yo-yo, starting with 180 grit abrasive and working down to 400 grit. Keep the abrasive underneath the revolving wood and move it from side to side continuously. Sand inside the slot as well to make it really smooth. Finish with a non-woven web pad. Remember to wear a dust mask and a visor when sanding and try to remove as much dust at source as possible by holding the nozzle of an extractor as close to the work as is practical.

8. Apply a coat of cellulose sanding sealer to all the surfaces, including the slot, using kitchen paper, and work quickly with the lathe stationary. De-nib with fine non-woven web and then repeat the whole process.

9. Apply a friction polish to the rotating wood to build up a high shine, and finish off with carnauba wax. Polish with a pad of kitchen paper.

10. When you remove the work from the

lathe you will notice that the drive and centre leave a ring mark and a centre-pop; you may also have a little burn mark in the centre caused by friction at the headstock end. If you are unhappy with these marks either cover them with a brass upholstery pin or turn up covers.

11. To turn a suitable cover mount a blank ¾ x ¾ x 4in (19 x 19 x 100mm) long between the centres and turn it to a diameter of ⅜in (18mm). With a small parting tool cut ¼in (6mm) spigots along the blank – as many as you require. Remove from the lathe and cut through each spigot with a fine saw. Remove the friction drive from the headstock and replace it with a small drill chuck. Chuck the spigot and turn the wood to form a flat-domed shape, which you can then sand, polish or colour. Drill a ¼in (6mm) hole where the drives have marked the wood, spread glue on the spigot and tap it gently into the hole with a soft-faced hammer.

Fig.130 Turning a one-piece yo-yo from a blank mounted between centres. A spindle gouge is used for the shaping and a parting tool for the centre slot.

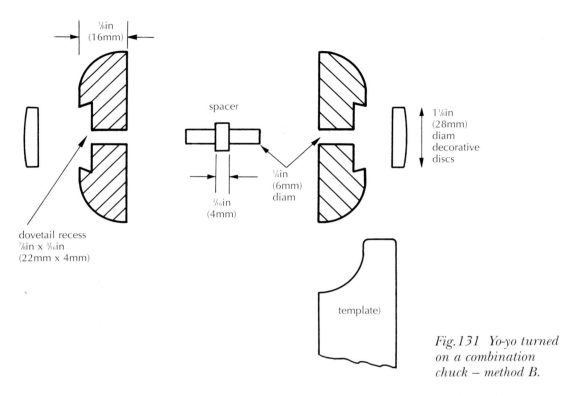

⅝in (16mm)

spacer

1⅛in (28mm) diam decorative discs

¼in (6mm) diam

3⁄16in (4mm)

dovetail recess
⅞in x 3⁄16in
(22mm x 4mm)

template)

Fig.131 Yo-yo turned on a combination chuck – method B.

12. Thread up the yo-yo with a proper twisted string, choose an area where you cannot do any damage, and away you go!

YO-YO TURNED ON A COMBINATION CHUCK

In this example the yo-yo is turned in three separate pieces as shown in Fig.131, with two fillers to decorate the dovetail recesses. More turning is involved but less wood is used.

Turning The Two Cheeks

1. Prepare two blanks of dense hardwood, such as box or holly, 2¾ x 2¾ x 1in (70 x 70 x 25mm), and mount one on a glue chuck.

Fit a revolving centre in the tailstock.

2. Turn the blank to the round 2⅜in (60mm) in diameter and face off. Cut a dovetail recess to suit your chuck jaws. Check that the jaws fit into the recess.

3. Draw a line ⅝in (16mm) from the outer edge, and with a thin parting tool make a cut to a depth of ¾in (19mm).

4. Bring up the tailstock with the revolving centre fitted to give support and then shape the blank with a spindle gouge. A small template for the curve of the outer shape is useful and will make it easier to get both cheeks the same.

5. Carefully sand and burnish the work well and then part off, cutting the final spigot through with a fine saw.

6. Turn the second cheek in exactly the same way.

Fig. 132 Turning one cheek of a yo-yo with a spindle gouge. The revolving centre is used to give additional support. The dovetail recess, ready for the chuck jaws, has already been turned.

Fig. 133 Measuring the centre spacer with callipers. The blank was painted red so that it could clearly be seen in the photograph which areas had been turned.

7. Now mount one of the blanks on to the chuck in expansion mode and make sure that the work revolves accurately. Always check that work mounted in dovetail jaws is in fact running true, either with the lathe running at slow speed or by rotating the headstock spindle by hand. A shaving, or some dust in the recess, may cause it to run off-true.

8. Turn the inner surface with a spindle gouge, a scraper or both, to give an absolutely smooth surface. It is important that this surface is smooth so that the cord will not catch, and to guarantee minimum friction. This method has an advantage over the previous method in this respect because you have complete access to smooth and polish the slot.

9. Sand and then apply cellulose sealer and friction polish.

10. Mount a drill chuck in the tailstock fitted with a sharp ¼in (6mm) diameter HSS twist drill and drill right through.

11. Remove the completed half from the lathe and repeat with the second cheek.

Turning The Central Spacer

1. Mount a blank using a matching hardwood, to the dimensions specified in Fig.131.

2. Turn the blank to the round and then form the ⅛in (3mm) wide spacer and the spigots.

3. Measure the spacer accurately using the callipers.

4. Cut through the spigots with a fine saw.

5. Glue the spacer into the two previously drilled holes in the cheeks.

Decoration

The last task is to turn two fillers, ¾in (19mm) in diameter and ⅛in (4mm) thick, to fill the dovetail recesses (the dimensions will differ with whichever chuck you are using). You can use any wood, maybe a darker or lighter one to give a contrast. There is plenty of scope for colouring the yo-yos with wood dyes, cutting decorative rings and making patterns and burning on names with a pyrography tool. There will be lots of ways you will come up with to make your yo-yo unique.

STRINGING

To make a string for a yo-yo take a length of string twice the length and half the thickness of the final desired length, and twist it many times. Keep the string taut whilst doing this. Next push the yo-yo spindle firmly against the middle of your twisted string and bring the two halves of the string together while maintaining the tension on them. When they meet let go of the yo-yo while holding the two free ends together. The yo-yo will spin as the two halves of the string wind around one another. Knot the free end firmly and make a finger loop. If you have put enough twists into the string in the first place the two halves should now have twisted together so firmly that they are indistinguishable from a single shorter piece of thicker string. The loop which passes over the spindle will grip firmly.

It is the precise degree of firmness of this grip, the friction between spindle and string, that determines the performance of the yo-yo, which is going to be a balance between the number of twists you have made and the finish you put on the spindle. If all that seems very complicated do as we did, and buy a packet of yo-yo strings from a toyshop and follow the simple diagram on the packet!

Project 7 – Table, Chairs and Stool for Teddies

The theme for this final project is a storybook one. The little rectangular table with its two chairs and stool is just the right size for teddy bears to sit at to have their breakfast porridge, or for dolls to have their tea parties. The table is influenced in design by a Victorian nursery table with simple turned legs. The two chairs are both the same size but Father Bear's chair has arms. The chairs

Fig.134 Table, chairs and stool.

7. Sand the leg well, burnish it and then remove it from the lathe.

8. Follow the same procedure for the remaining three legs, using the turning guide in each case to ensure that the Vs are accurately plotted but using the first leg as a guide for the diameters.

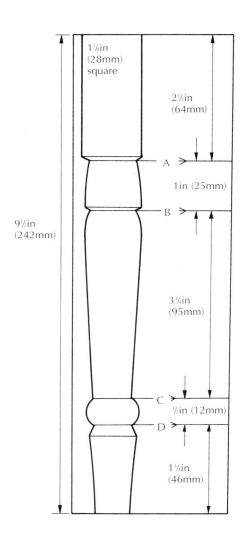

Fig. 136 Turning guide for the table leg.

CONSTRUCTING THE TOP

Cut out the two pieces to make the table top. With a plane true up the two long edges, which are going to be glued together. The boards should fit together without any gaps. Apply PVA adhesive to one edge and rub the two pieces of wood together to ensure a good spread of glue. Wipe off any excess and then cramp up the boards to dry overnight. If your bench is fitted with bench 'dogs' these are ideal for this operation. Put a sheet of paper between the bench and the gluing boards to stop adhesion to the bench, and apply central, downward pressure to reduce any risk of bowing. A heavy weight, or a brick wrapped in paper, will help here. Some woods have a marked tendency to bow, and you may therefore decide not to glue the edges together. Remove the top from the bench and sand the edges smooth. If you have a router you can mould the edges and then lightly sand to round off the arises; if not, plane a slight chamfer around the edge to reduce the risk of damage and to remove any sharp edges.

MAKING THE FRAME

1. Cut the four pieces that make up the frame and make sure the ends are all absolutely square. The lower arises should be gently rounded or moulded with a router. Because the wood we used was not very strong, compared with beech for example, we decided to use proprietary dowels rather than mortise and tenon joints. Note in the cutting list that you will need longer frame pieces if you are going to put the frame together with mortise and tenon joints. Full instructions on dowelling are given in Chapter 7.

Fig.137 The two table-top pieces have been glued together and the surface has been planed and sanded. The picture shows the end vice in the bench and the metal dogs being used to form a clamp for the gluing up stage. The wood marked with cross hatching is used as a packing piece to ensure that the two pieces of wood are supported by the flat area of the bench. The piece of white paper underneath the wood is to stop the glue marking the nice new bench!

Fig.138 Assembling the table using the dowelling technique.

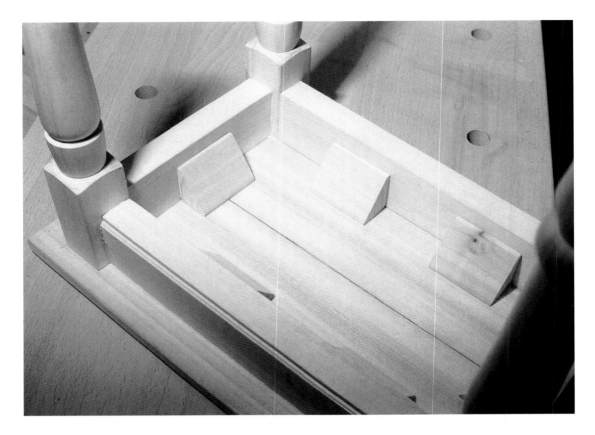

Fig.139 Glue blocks are used to strengthen the bond between the frame and the underside of the top.

2. Drill the holes for the dowels so that they do not interfere with one another, as follows. The two short frame pieces (A) have one hole drilled in each end, and the two long frame pieces (B) have two dowel holes drilled in each end. In all case the holes are drilled with a ⅜in (8mm) diameter drill bit to a depth of 1in (25mm).

3. On the underside of the table top carefully mark out the positions for the frame and legs.

4. Glue and cramp the two short frame pieces (A) to the underside of the table top. When holding wood, either in the drill

press or in a vice, and when cramping up, it is good practice to protect the surface of the wood with scraps of hardwood and to line the jaw faces of metal vices with offcuts of plywood or hardwood.

5. Whilst the glue cures, accurately mark the position on each leg, using the dowelling points, where the two dowel holes need to be drilled to match those in the long frame pieces (B). Drill these holes as before to be ⅜in (8mm) in diameter and 1in (25mm) deep. Dowel the legs to the long frame pieces and cramp up. Wipe away any glue that oozes out with a damp cloth before it stains the wood.

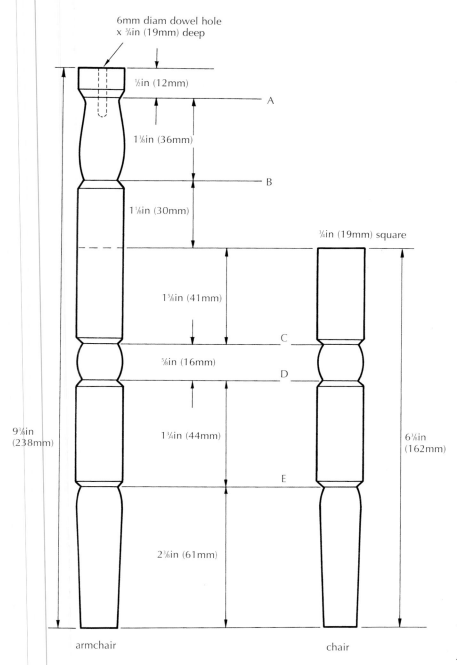

6mm diam dowel hole
x ¾in (19mm) deep

½in (12mm)

A

1⅜in (36mm)

B

1⅛in (30mm)

¾in (19mm) square

1⅝in (41mm)

C

⅝in (16mm)

D

1¾in (44mm)

E

9⅜in
(238mm)

6⅜in
(162mm)

2⅜in (61mm)

armchair

chair

Fig.140
Turning guide
for the chair legs.

Fig.153 Stencilling a motif on the side of the table. Transfers are probably much easier to apply!

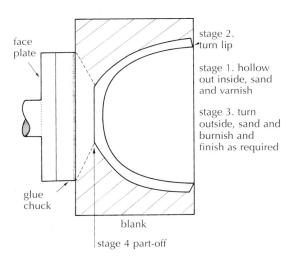

face
plate

stage 2.
turn lip

stage 1. hollow
out inside, sand
and varnish

stage 3. turn
outside, sand and
burnish and
finish as required

glue
chuck

blank

stage 4 part-off

Fig.154 Porridge bowls.

1. Following the stages in the drawing in Fig.154, use a small ¼in (6mm) spindle gouge and hollow out the inside of the blank. Sand and burnish.
2. Turn the lip of the bowl.
3. Turn the outside shape of the bowl. The wall thickness will be determined by the wood that is chosen and the skill of the turner. Sand and burnish and apply any finish at this stage.
4. Part off, undercutting the base slightly so that the bowl sits without rocking.
5. Repeat the process for the middle-sized bowl, commencing with a blank 3 x 2in (76 x 50mm) thick, and then turn the smallest bowl from a blank 2½ x 2in thick (64 x 50mm). The three bowls should stack inside one another.

Fig.155 Turning a small bowl using a spindle gouge with the blank held on a glue chuck. The lathe being used is the APTC Carbatec.

SPOONS

1. Turn the spoons from three hardwood blanks measuring 5 x 1 x 1in (127 x 25 x 25mm).
2. Mount a blank between centres. Mark off ⅛in (6mm) each end and leave this as waste wood to be cut off at the end of turning, as shown in Fig.157. Turn the handle of the spoon to a diameter of ⅛in (6mm) and with a length of 2⅜in (64mm). Turn the remaining wood to an egg shape to form the bowl of the spoon.
3. Turn off the lathe. Lock the headstock if this is possible on your lathe and, using

155

LIST OF SUPPLIERS

Liberon Waxes Ltd
Mountfield Industrial Works
Learoyd Road
New Romney
Kent
TN28 8XU
Tel: 01797 367555

● Products widely stocked by tool retailers.

Lovell Workwear
44 Heol Powis
Birchgrove
Cardiff
CF4 4PH
Tel: 01222 618112

● Smocks and aprons.
● Mail order service.

Multistar Machine & Tool Ltd
Unit B5
Cowdray Centre
Cowdray Avenue
Colchester
CO1 1BL
Tel: 01206 549944

● Titan and Duplex chucks and accessories.
● Brochure available.
● Mail order service.

Record Power
Parkway Works
Sheffield
S9 3BL
Tel: 0114 2449066

● Manufacturer of lathes and wood-working machinery. Available through accredited dealers.

Rexon Ltd
Barbot Hall Industrial Estate
Rotherham
S. Yorks
S61 4RJ
Tel: 01709 361158

● Manufacturer of lathes and wood-working machinery. Available through accredited dealers.

Severnply
14 Gloucester Road
Stonehouse
Gloucestershire
Tel: 01453 826886

● Large selection of birch plywood and man-made boards.

Index